THE
CHURCH
CREATIVE

THE
CHURCH
CREATIVE

*A Reader on
the Renewal of the Church*

Edited by

*M. Edward Clark
William L. Malcomson
Warren Lane Molton*

ABINGDON PRESS
Nashville and New York

THE CHURCH CREATIVE

Copyright © 1967 by Abingdon Press

Library of Congress Catalog Card Number: 67-22157

Scripture quotations unless otherwise noted are from the Revised Standard
Version of the Bible, copyrighted 1946 and 1952 by the Division of Christian
Education, National Council of Churches, and are used by permission.

Scripture quotations noted NEB are from the New English Bible, New
Testament, © the Delegates of the Oxford University Press and the Syndics
of the Cambridge University Press, 1961. Reprinted by permission.

The article "New-Look Church in California," pp. 80-86 is copyright 1966
by *Presbyterian Life* and is used by permission of that journal.

SET UP, PRINTED, AND BOUND BY THE
PARTHENON   PRESS,   AT   NASHVILLE,
TENNESSEE, UNITED STATES OF AMERICA

To the students of
Central Baptist Theological Seminary

FOREWORD

We live in a world of rapid change, change in the forms, methods, and values of life. There is in us a great ambivalence toward this change. We can be fascinated participants in the contemporary developments and movements that are producing change, and yet we can also draw back and be afraid of leaving the old ways and values and fear the new which only gradually reveals its characteristics. This ambivalence is especially true of church life and is naturally reflected in the attitudes of both clergy and laity.

The Church Creative strikes effective blows at this ambivalence and demonstrates how the balance of church life can be tipped on the side of creative experimentation involving both clergy and laity. Here is a book that describes in plain terms how churches can explore the expanding frontiers of the church's ministry. There are interesting descriptions of all kinds of experiments: in education, pastoral care, and group life; in the training and direction of the ministry of the laity; in implementing the church's responsibility for the world; in the use of art and other human resources; in the design of worship and the development of reconciling relationships.

I am impressed that most of the authors have been very practical in their approach. First, they describe the experiment; second, they formulate the principles of procedure that can be used by the reader in his own situation.

There is much talk today about the importance of the church's finding new forms for its ministry. The authors of this book supply eighteen examples of new forms that will excite the reader's imagination. Vitality is always fashioning new forms and changing old ones. There is evidence in these descriptions of the Spirit's work in guiding people into new ways of ministry. These ways provide a means for cooperation between man and God for the forming of the church creative.

REUEL L. HOWE

PREFACE

The story is "going the rounds" that the local congregation, the parish church is, if not dead, at least terminally ill. There have been a spate of books diagnosing the illness. These books have sometimes been descriptive, sometimes moralistic or normative, and sometimes satirical. Chastening though such books have been, they have served a useful purpose in tearing from the eyes of many Christians the rose-colored glasses through which they have viewed the church.

One of the effects of these books, however, has been to convince some people that the only places where anything is happening of consequence are outside the structure of the local congregation. Or, if there are congregations doing significant work, these are quite unusual, avant-garde situations which seem remote to most of us.

It is the conviction of the editors of this volume that along with such books as *The Comfortable Pew, How to Become a Bishop Without Being Religious, The Suburban Captivity of the Churches,* to mention only a few, there is now a need to publicize more widely some of the ministries that are taking place in areas where people are taking the claims of the Christian faith with seriousness. The essays in this volume are intended as evidences of creative ministry. They are not intended as examples of "how to do it." They are presented here in the hope that they may encourage others, both laity and clergy, to seek to minister creatively, experimentally, even daringly in the particular and peculiar situation in which they are located.

9

If there are insights coming forth from the new bursts of creativity in the church, certainly one of these is that every local situation is unique and that mass programs planned in denominational headquarters seldom hit the mark. This book then is not intended to give "answers," but to stimulate the search for ministries *with* people in the world, including those who are outside as well as those inside the institutional church.

The essays presented are only representative of much that is happening in the churches of America. It would be misleading to infer, however, that any large number of churches of any denomination or of all denominations put together have been imbued with the desire to minister creatively to the needs of the world. The percentage is still small. It is too soon even to suggest that these few represent the beginning of a trend. The ministries, of which these essays are only representative, may or may not be the first bold ripples of the "wave of the future." Even so, the editors feel they have a contribution to make to the church as it seeks to find itself in the sixties of the twentieth century.

M. EDWARD CLARK
WILLIAM L. MALCOMSON
WARREN LANE MOLTON

ACKNOWLEDGMENTS

We are very grateful to all the writers who have contributed to the making of this book. They, not the editors, are the creative persons. In every case the writing has been undertaken as a task over and above many other responsibilities. A special word of appreciation is due to Dr. Reuel L. Howe who was gracious enough to write the Foreword, even though he was engaged in writing a new book of his own. The editors are in the debt also of Mrs. M. Edward Clark, Mrs. William McBride, and Mrs. Bill L. Shook for their secretarial assistance, not only for the typing of the manuscript but for much of the correspondence as well.

It must be understood, too, that the book would not have been made possible apart from the encouragement of President Paul T. Losh and Dean Robert G. Torbet of the Central Baptist Theological Seminary, and their desire to have members of the seminary faculty engage in a project of this nature.

CONTENTS

1

Girding Laity for Mission

Kenneth W. Conners

Is renewal possible within the structure of the conventional
city church? Can a church which has been called a "cathedral
of Methodism" really become relevant to the needs of a changing urban parish? Can its laity be mobilized, molded into lay
ministers, and motivated to go "on mission"—ministering to
the world in a truly compassionate outreach? Can the church
thus move out of its ecclesiastical bomb shelter and risk its
life by becoming a reconciling force in the midst of tension,
strife, and suffering? Or is it necessary to start fresh, un-
hampered by tradition, unfettered by existing structures, as
did Washington's unique Church of the Saviour?

These are the sort of questions which confronted the First
Methodist Church of Germantown in Philadelphia as it entered
the secular sixties and anxiously contemplated its uncertain
future. The questions were not academic. The church found
itself facing some hard facts which called for hard decisions.

The membership, for example, which had climbed to almost
two thousand during World War II, had been gradually
deteriorating ever since the war-imposed ban on home building
was lifted. As local residents migrated to the suburbs and the
church rolls dropped month after month, the character of the
neighborhood steadily changed. Old mansions were converted
into apartments. An influx of Negroes brought dark faces to

15

former all-white blocks. Although the church was located some seven miles from the center of Philadelphia, virtually all the complex problems of the city—physical deterioration, neighborhood tensions, increasing crime, traffic congestion—could be found in this uptown-downtown parish.

Each year inflation and the increasing maintenance needed for the 2.2 million dollar church property pushed up the budget. Each year it became more difficult to eke out the last thousands of dollars in pledges needed to underwrite expenses. At official board meetings discussion inevitably would gravitate to the latest church statistics, followed by gloomy predictions of further decline.

Nevertheless, all was not hopeless. Despite losses to the suburbs, First Methodist still had fourteen hundred members, and they comprised a remarkably loyal, diverse group of creative, concerned people. There were Ph.D.'s and grammar school graduates, executives and clerks, liberals and conservatives, a few Negro members and one or two Orientals. The church, too, had a reputation for a distinguished pulpit where basic issues, popular and unpopular, were fully discussed; a ministry of music which maintained high standards; services notable for a reverent spirit of worship. Moreover, the extensive church property was admirably suited for a seven-day-a-week program.

This, then, was the situation at the hour of decision. Should the church follow the flight to the suburbs, sell its present buildings to a Negro congregation, purchase a well-located ten-acre tract, and construct a new edifice where parking would be convenient, new member prospects plentiful, and the church's future bright? Or should the congregation stand its ground, seek ministerial leadership capable of training the laity for a new kind of outreach to the city environment, and get involved in the often-turbulent crosscurrents of the urban milieu?

The decision to stay became a commitment, in the spring

of 1961, when Robert A. Raines agreed to come from Cleveland, Ohio, to serve First Methodist, Germantown. Author of *New Life in the Church,* he believed that the real battleground of the church—the place where Protestantism must stand or fall—is the city. It is here that tensions are great, that key decisions are made, that a cross section of people and problems and potential for service exists. If the church is to become relevant, he felt, it must learn how to minister not only to the well-to-do, but to the disenchanted, the lonely, the underprivileged—the very people served by Christ in his ministry.

From this point forward, the strategy of First Methodist was based on four somewhat unusual propositions:

First, the lay members of the church would have to be trained "in depth." This would involve personal instruction and development of a scope seldom attempted in a large church. It would require that the laity come to grips with the basic beliefs of Christianity, facing honestly their doubts and uncertainties, and not being expected to subscribe to tenets which force them to compromise their integrity, yet striving continually to grow in spiritual sensitivity and perceptiveness, all the while laying the groundwork for whatever form of witness their particular talents might make possible.

Second, ways would have to be found of reaching and serving creatively two segments of society which have written off the church as a factor in their lives—written it off because it so often seems to be a smug fellowship of those who have "arrived," a fellowship quick to pass judgment on "outsiders," a fellowship almost neurotically concerned with preserving its status, its security, its exclusiveness. One of the groups thus alienated comprises the artist, the musician, the writer and dramatist, and many men of science. They have turned their backs on the conventional church. The other group is composed of people who need help and understanding in time of need, a protagonist in time of injustice. They feel the church

17

has turned its back on them. Much as the late Pope John XXIII threw open the windows of the Vatican, First Methodist had to find ways of opening its doors, both as a means of entry and as an access route to the outside world for those bent on mission.

Third, to develop this kind of lay-training, lay-mission program would require not just one, but two senior ministers— two men with requisite skills, experience, and creativity. Obviously, this would necessitate a larger salary budget than is provided by churches of comparable size which have one senior minister and one or more assistants. First Methodist would have to be willing and able to underwrite such an expenditure.

Fourth, the church would refuse to play the "numbers game." It would not strive to build up membership or budgets or programs on the false premise that "bigness" is a true measure of religious strength and vitality. Rather, stress would be placed on *quality* of commitment. It would be recognized that a smaller, leaner body of Christ might be more responsive, more dedicated, more effective in its ministry than one burdened with an excess of spiritual flabbiness. It was recognized, too, that some members of the church family might find such an approach more appalling than appealing. As a result, those willing to commit themselves to some form of discipline and mission might constitute only a portion of the total membership. This fact, and the inevitable mistakes of judgment which would occur from time to time, would create a continuing risk that some folk might become disenchanted and withdraw their support of the church.

To put this strategy into operation and get more "senior ministerial" strength, the church decided to try a co-ministry. In the spring of 1962, from New Rochelle, New York, came Theodore W. Loder, who had known Bob Raines at Yale Divinity School and was receptive to the co-ministry idea. Vitally interested in church-community cooperative action, Mr.

Loder and his experience and background have nicely comple-
mented that of Mr. Raines. The third member of the young,
creative team is Jared J. Rardin, who became associate minister
upon his graduation from New York City's Union Theological
Seminary in June, 1963. Mr. Rardin's year of internship at
Washington's Church of the Saviour has proved of value
to a church like First Methodist which seeks to intensify the
spirit of discipleship among its members.

With the preaching divided almost equally between Mr.
Raines and Mr. Loder, except for those Sundays—perhaps six
a year—when Mr. Rardin occupies the pulpit, each week finds
one of the co-ministers relieved of sermon preparation. This
frees each of some twenty to twenty-five hours for other activities. In much the same way, administrative duties are divided
between the two men, with corresponding savings in senior
ministerial time. The co-ministry also lends itself to occasional
dialogue sermons in which theological, pastoral, or social issues
are batted back and forth between pulpit and lectern to the
delight of the congregation which continues to look upon
Sunday morning worship as central and basic to the spiritual
vitality of the church. The co-ministers also benefit by consulting
with each other on pastoral and theological problems, and
by interchanging advice, encouragement, and constructive
critiques.

Gains such as these are not without cost, however. Even
when two men trust each other, respect each other's abilities,
have affection for each other, tensions can develop of a type
familiar to every business executive. Someone has said that
co-ministers must learn to practice mutual subordination, and
that is true. There are times when each man literally must
struggle to suppress his natural inclination to want to dominate,
to be in the limelight, to receive a major share of the congregation's approval and affection. In these and other areas involving
personal fulfillment, Mr. Rardin serves as a valuable ministerial

catalyst by providing a mature, impartial ministry to both men.

With an unusual depth of professional leadership available, the training of the laity could go forward on a broad front. Significantly, new members are exposed to it even before they join the church. Twice yearly a "Christian Faith and Life" class is held for the thirty-five to forty-five people who are interested in membership. Meeting one night weekly for six weeks, this course includes on its "faculty" not only the ministers, but laymen as well. An hour before the new people are due to arrive, ministers and lay trainers meet to share in a worship-litany, to discuss the subject matter to be covered that evening, to interchange ideas and insights, and to pray that they may become channels for the Holy Spirit to touch the lives of others. By the time this preparatory period ends, ministers and laymen alike feel the excitement of imminent personal encounter with new friends.

Each session opens with devotions led by one of the lay trainers. As scriptural passages are read and the layman speaks of the relevance of the words to situations we encounter today —often citing incidents from his life in which these particular verses have "come alive"—members of the class are noticeably moved. For some, it is a surprise to find a lay person, and not a minister, conducting such a worship service. For others, it is a new experience to hear a church member speak of his faith so freely, so eloquently, with such an absence of self-consciousness.

For the next half-hour one of the ministers discusses the topic of the evening. This may be "Renewal of the Church: Mission," "Jesus Christ," "Life Together," "The Good News: Freedom and Forgiveness," or similar themes dealing with the basics of the Christian faith. The prospective new members then are divided into groups of twelve to fifteen people. Each group is taken to a different room for a discussion period, led by two of the lay trainers and based on material presented in the talk. The lay persons—a man and a woman—serve not only as discussion leaders for the duration of the course but, in a larger sense, as spiritual "shepherds" of the people in their particular "flocks."

On the first night each of the new people is asked to introduce himself, to say something about his religious background, his vocation, what led him to come to First Methodist, as well as anything he cares to volunteer about his spiritual quest. From this initial experience of getting acquainted and from continuing participation, week after week, in discussions which lead people to share with remarkable candor their innermost hopes and fears, a sense of Christian community begins to develop. Members of the group begin to know one another more intimately, more sympathetically, than has been the case with friends of long acquaintance. Because they have come together, not as social or economic or ethnic "clans," but out of a common desire to experience firsthand the good news that Christ proclaims, many long-accepted value-judgments begin to crumble. "Ordinary" people are found to be quite "extraordinary"; "different" people on closer scrutiny do not appear to be really so different. Before long, many in the group become uncomfortably aware of the myopic, distorted eyes through which they have been gazing at, but not really seeing, their fellowman. When the time of decision arrives, they come into the larger fellowship not as strangers, but as friends who already are becoming united in what Martin Buber has called "I-Thou" relationships.

Always there are a few who decide not to join. This causes no anxiety on the part of the lay trainers, for throughout the course it is made clear that membership is not the sole objective; both new people and present members of the church are welcome if, by their presence, the imperatives of Christianity have become more real to them.

The reasons for not joining, however, are usually interesting. Some feel that membership may involve more of a commitment than they are ready to undertake. Others feel that the course has raised questions in their minds without giving them all the answers. Actually these people may be in the process of rejecting, for the first time, some of the parochial beliefs of their childhood and are having the frightening experience of groping, firsthand, for answers to the probing questions raised by the Gospels. Often these people repeat the course, six months later, and then join the church, feeling they can now seek to grow in grace in a spirit of excitement and joy.

Ted Loder likes to say, mischievously, "It's easier to become a minister of this church than to become a member. I'm glad I got in as a minister. I doubt if I could have made it otherwise!"

Many who join First Methodist clamor to go into a koinonia group. Composed of twelve to fifteen people who meet biweekly in various homes for devotions, Bible study, and the sharing of experiences and concerns, koinonia groups enable people to study on a programmed basis, to learn to know other people in depth, to share in their joys and sorrows, to pray for common concerns—in short, within the structure of a large church, to experience the fellowship of a small, committed group of Christians who seek to minister to one another. Some koinonia groups function for months, others for years, depending upon the needs of the particular group. As a means of deepening spiritual sensitivity through personal participation leading to self-awareness, they serve a valuable purpose.

Also helpful in developing a lay sense of community awareness and commitment are retreats. Each year First Methodist schedules four or five weekend retreats for adults at Kirkridge, in the Pocono Mountains of Pennsylvania. Occasional retreats also are held for teen-agers, led by Jerry Rardin, as well as day retreats for women's groups at places in the metropolitan Philadelphia area. The isolation from the distractions of modern living gives retreatants an opportunity to focus intensively on specific concerns such as deepening the dimensions of prayer life or seeking ways of ministering to the needs of the community. Another stimulus to lay development is frequent lectures, forums, and seminars. A series of meetings on "Renewal in Religious Life," for example, brought Dr. Martin Marty to speak on Protestant renewal trends, Monsignor Philip Dowling to speak on Catholic renewal, and Rabbi Theodore Gordon to discuss Jewish renewal. Theological doctrine is reviewed in lectures such as were given by Dr. Claude Welch on the Trinity. A six-week seminar based on Bonhöffer's *Ethics,* given by Professor William H. Lazareth of the Lutheran Seminary, examined the application of Christian principles. New theological concepts have been expounded by men like Bishop John Robinson of *Honest to God* fame, the moral aspects of political policies by speakers like Senator Joseph Clark, the unrest on the college campus by Chaplain William Sloane Coffin, Jr., of Yale University, the needs of the secular city by Dr. Harvey Cox, the complex aspects of race relations by the Reverend Andrew Young, strategist for Dr. Martin Luther King.

Emphasis, too, is placed on the reading of significant current books. Last year the church's bookstore sold more than two thousand dollars worth of books—many of them inexpensive paperbacks—on theology, ethics, prayer, pastoral psychology, biblical interpretation, social concerns. The circulating library kept other volumes in continual use.

A related project is the booklet of Lenten meditations, sent to all First Methodist members early every February. Instead of the church's purchasing booklets from some publisher, forty people in the congregation are asked to choose a text, write a personal meditation, and a suitable prayer. This not only requires the contributor to redefine some aspect of his faith and reduce it to writing, but produces a devotional Lenten guide which gets wide readership by members of the parish who are interested in the meditations of other lay people.

These, then, are some of the ways in which First Methodist seeks to equip its people for their ministry in the world. But what of that ministry? What forms is it taking? How are a people who always have been mission-minded, in the institutional sense, now experimenting with personal forms of mission closer to home?

One of the first innovations proposed by Mr. Raines, shortly after his arrival in Germantown, was aimed at turning the congregation's gaze toward the needs of the immediate neighborhood. It involved Turner Chapel, a magnificent Gothic structure used for the early Sunday worship service and for an occasional wedding or memorial service. Throughout the week its doors and the doors of the main sanctuary were locked. Let's open the chapel twenty-four hours daily for prayer, suggested Mr. Raines.

The proposal aroused many fears. What of vandalism to a building valued at $750,000? Or the danger of assaults on visitors to the chapel? Installation of an automatic alarm system provided protection for the people; so this left only the risk of damage to a valuable structure and the pertinent question: Is this building to be revered and shut off from the world, or is it a sacred place only when it is serving *people—all* people of the community, at any hour of the day or night?

Proper precautions were taken, and the church officials gamely agreed to go along, but with some skepticism as to whether the chapel actually would be used late at night. After a few months an actual count showed as many as two hundred visits monthly between 7:00 P.M. and 2:00 A.M. Some were nurses going to, or returning from, Germantown Hospital. Some were people on their way home from parties. Others were just passersby who saw the lights and obeyed an impulse to go in. This innovation, then, became one symbol of First Methodist's desire to serve its neighbors. Significantly, at a recent Christian Faith and Life class, one new member trainee observed that his first contact with the church was through using the chapel for prayer. "It was the only Protestant place of worship in all of Germantown I could find open at night," he said. "It meant a lot to me. I think the church of Christ should always have open doors."

From that day onward, more and more of First Methodist's doors swung open. For example, more than a score of the church's members now spend one night each week tutoring high-school youngsters—most of them Negroes—who troop through the doors of the church's educational building seeking to improve their scholastic standing and thus avoiding becoming dropouts. Many of the tutors belong to koinonia groups, using this form of outreach as their "mission."

On Friday evenings sixty to seventy young people crowd into The Glass Door, a teen-age snack shop also in the educational building. Sitting at candlelighted tables, sipping coffee and Cokes, munching cookies and cakes, and surrounded by displays of art, these teen-agers—many of them culturally deprived—listen to folk singers, jazz combos, dramatic skits, and talks on a variety of subjects. The skits and talks are designed to stir up the sort of discussion which brings young people face-to-face with ethical and social issues. Mr. Rardin, who is largely responsible for "The Glass Door," staffs it with a group of young adults who meet regularly in a koinonia context.

The doors swung open for the artist, the poet, the musician, the writer, the playwright, when the church staged its first Religious Arts Festival, several years ago. Sparked by Dr. W. Lawrence Curry, minister of music, and his talented wife, Louise, and involving the dedicated work of scores of the church's creative lay people, the three-day festival presented a large gallery of religious paintings, prints, sculpture, and stained glass from Philadelphia's professional artists and studios; additional art by the church's own artists, adult and juvenile; plays produced by a New York City troupe; a performance of

Randall Thompson's *Peaceable Kingdom* by an interracial, interdenominational chorus conducted by the composer; and seminars on art, literature, drama, the dance, and creative forms of Christian education. So successful was the festival that a second and even more comprehensive version was presented two years later. It seems destined to become a biennial event, appealing to people who perhaps have not been inside a church for years.

One outgrowth of the festival was the formation of a "Listening to the World" group by Mr. Loder. Aimed at increasing the sensitivity of church people to what the novelist, the playwright, and the poet are saying about life in our contemporary society, these reading and discussion sessions became so popular that a second group had to be formed. Another outgrowth of the festival was the formation of a Fine Arts Committee, which sponsors dramatic productions, film festivals, and other presentations. Mr. Loder has said: "God is speaking to us, not just through the theologian, but through the artist as well. If the church chooses not to listen to the artist, it will be deaf to a significant part of God's word in our time."

Down at Covenant House, some ten blocks south of the church in a tension-filled, interracial neighborhood, two young women—members of the church—live in a second-floor apartment, providing a form of outreach which might be called an "apostolate of being there." Below, in a large room, a preschool class of four-year-olds meets three days weekly for instruction by an accredited teacher and assistant. During the late afternoon some ten adults are tutoring a score of older youngsters. There is a library as well as recreational facilities for the "club"— children who pour into Covenant House on certain scheduled days. An adjacent room is a medical office in which one of the young women, who is a pediatrician, ministers to the community.

Although Covenant House has no official connection with First Methodist, its existence stemmed from action by ten members of the church: the two young women, who had intended offering their skills in foreign service but came to realize that great need existed close at hand; the other eight, who agreed to help make this possible. The covenant that was evolved provided for weekly meetings of the group for Bible study and prayer, common involvement in whatever project might develop, monthly giving of a self-imposed assessment, and continuing support of First Methodist, through which the ten persons had come to know one another. Within a few months a house was found and purchased and the interior renovated at the expense of aching backs. No social service agency, Covenant House is an experiment in personal ministry, one that has attracted gifts of money, time, and talents from Protestants, Catholics, and even so-called atheists.

Personal witness by First Methodist people takes many forms. One man, a business executive, invited factory and office workers interested in improving human relations to meet in his office at noontime for lunch, study of the Bible or contemporary books, and discussion. At one time three different groups were meeting weekly, developing within that company a needed spirit of reconciliation.

Another businessman, sent by his firm to South Africa to determine what wage rates should be established for workers to be employed in a new plant under construction, was distressed by the low level of going rates and the wretched living conditions. While flying back to America he wrote his "sermon" —a report advocating higher-than-usual rates so that workers could live decently. His Christian concern was heard by top management, which gave its approval.

Other members travel to near or distant points to occupy pulpits as guest preachers, to lead retreats, to help organize koinonia groups, to speak to organizations interested in fostering lay activity. Women of the church visit patients in mental institutions, in hospitals, and in convalescent homes, often taking one of the church's tape recorders so shut-ins can hear sermonettes by their pastors and choral music.

This glimpse of "new life" in one church should not imply unqualified success in all programs undertaken. Inevitably any exciting, experimental form of urban ministry makes mistakes and creates frustrating problems. It offends some people, especially those who have grown up in the institutional church. It disturbs some people, particularly those who feel the church must guard, at all costs, its dignity, its prestige, its status. It alienates some people, particularly those who feel that the status quo must be preserved even in the face of sweeping social changes. Nevertheless, it attracts other people, particularly those who have felt the guilt of Christianity when it has failed to follow its Christ without reserve and compromise.

As Harvey Cox, author of *The Secular City*, so sensitively points out, such a ministry draws into the church idealistic and eager young people of all ages who have become disenchanted with older, more pious forms of the church. At the same time it stirs up those who came into the church years ago and now feel that the rules have been changed while the game still is in progress.

Thus, First Methodist and other churches striving to become relevant to our times face a difficult dichotomy of ministry, if they are to serve all their people. They must, on the one hand, respond to the urging of the Holy Spirit and open up new areas to God's light and power. And they must, at the same time, find ways of providing a compassionate, understanding ministry to those who have given their talents, their gifts— indeed, the best years of their lives—to the church of Christ down through the decades.

This, perhaps, represents one of the greatest challenges we face today.

2

Interfaith Commission on Labor Relations

Raymond C. Phibbs

I cannot remember just when the Torrington area Interfaith Commission on Labor-Management Relations came into existence. I believe it was some time in 1961, though I have no records to prove it. It really does not matter, except to show how little significance any of us attached to the commission's creation at the time. Indeed, there was little reason to get excited or to expect very much. At the time it seemed to be nothing more than a belated and ineffectual expression of the concern of a few churchmen in a crisis which they had done nothing to prevent and in which they seemed powerless to help.

The churchmen of the Torrington area had every reason to be concerned, for everybody knew perfectly well that we were in a time of community crisis that was shaking the economic foundations of this industrial center of northwestern Connecticut. Torrington's economy had already suffered a couple of major body blows, and at the time we felt that even greater blows would soon fall. It would not be exaggerating to say that the community was close to panic, for I can well remember a long black-bordered editorial on the front page of a local newspaper urging people not to panic and not to start fleeing the area like rats leaving a sinking ship. While things looked black just now, the editorial went on, this was not the end of the line for Torrington, and prosperity would surely return someday.

It has. In 1967, with everything bustling and bursting with growth, it is hard to remember those dark days of six short years ago and even harder to admit that we were close to panic and hysteria. But we were. In order to appreciate that crisis which precipitated the establishment of the Interfaith Commission on Labor-Management Relations, let me sketch in a bit of local geography and history.

Torrington is a city of thirty thousand along the Naugatuck River in the Litchfield Hills of northwestern Connecticut. Like so many other Connecticut communities, its life is built around metal fabricating plants and precision tool and equipment industries. The manufacturing of needles, bearings, ice skates, kitchen utensils, timing devices, machine tools, and brass and copper tubing provides almost all the area's income.

The first great body blow to Torrington's economy was the incredible industrial comeback of Germany and Japan after World War II. By the mid-fifties the competition from these two sources was beginning to take a toll in sales of local products. One response was for large industries with branch plants to begin to consolidate and to eliminate their oldest, most inefficient, and obsolete plants. One such plant that got the ax was the local brass fabricating factory. For generations it had been an important part of the industrial backbone of Torrington. Its factories sprawled through the heart of the downtown area, and as many as a thousand Torrington families derived their income from "The Brass Mill."

In public statements the management of the parent company reported that it had no alternative but to phase out the Torrington operation and try to transfer as many workers as possible to other Connecticut cities where they had newer facilities and more efficient operations.

Torrington was still reeling from this loss when it became

30

more apparent that the largest company in the area, which employed over two thousand persons, was having its troubles also. Germany was pouring precision products onto the world market at prices that local industries were hard put to match. This largest of Torrington's industries, with several plants in other states and countries, began to consolidate its manufacturing operations. This did not affect Torrington at first because the home offices and plants of the company were in Torrington. However, as the competitive bind became tighter, the company was forced to deal with the fact that some of its oldest and most obsolete plants were right next door to its home offices and that some of its highest paid workers were in Torrington.

Another unpleasant fact that would not go away was that there was a history of labor-management conflict in Torrington. Justified or not (and local leaders maintained vehemently that it was *not* justified), the reputation of Torrington around the state was one of a "bad labor town." I have no way of knowing whether this was true or not, for I have never worked in labor-management relations outside the Torrington area. Nevertheless, the reputation was there.

As a few of the smaller stores on Main Street began to close their doors and as an out-of-town-owned department store began to move out, Torrington residents began to talk about the downtown area looking like a ghost town, and their sense of impending doom deepened as the rumors raced around town that two of Torrington's industries were considering closing their Torrington operation because production costs were too great.

The community began to take arms against a sea of troubles by putting pressure on the Connecticut legislature and administration until a new four-lane super highway was promised for the area. The bankrupt New Haven Railroad had long since ceased to provide passenger service up the Naugatuck, and the twisting two-lane roads through the hills were no incentive to new industry. The promise of a new highway brightened us all, but the question haunted us: Is it too little and too late? Many had the same mixed emotions when local leaders arranged for the building of a modern shopping plaza in downtown Torrington to lure shoppers and their money from Hartford and Waterbury. When a few, small electronic and textile industries moved into Torrington in response to local government and commercial efforts, everyone was pleased. Nevertheless, all of these, good as they were, were not enough. *The* number one question was: Could Torrington keep the large industrial base it now had? If a "Yes" could not be found to that question, it would be ultimately fruitless to provide solutions to any other problems.

By now, well aware that Torrington was "at the end of the line" as far as transportation and other factors so desirable for new industry were concerned, and increasingly aware of the very serious bind that Torrington industries found themselves in between increasing foreign and domestic competition and rising production costs, the residents of the area became aware of the third great factor in the gloomy picture—the so-called labor climate. In 1961 it became apparent that there was a serious difference between management and labor leaders in Torrington's major industry. Just what the differences were, no one beyond the negotiating teams seemed to know. But something was beginning to boil that had simmered for a long time.

A strike seemed inevitable just at the moment when the community could least afford it. There were many public calls for restraint and responsibility from various civic organizations printed in the newspaper alongside the charges and countercharges of union and management negotiators. One such call for reason and restraint came from the Protestant clergymen of the city. Later, we were to find out what effect that clerical plea had upon the ones who bore the responsibility for negotiations.

At the eleventh hour terms of a new two-year contract were agreed upon, and a strike was averted—but not before the public was made aware that such conflict with labor could be a major factor in management's decision whether or not to close its two-thousand man operation in Torrington. Such a possibility, sounding the death knell of the economic life of Torrington, made men shudder. It also made them highly partisan. The prolabor people saw the heartless Goliath using great power to destroy and eventually kill the much less powerful unions. Those inclined to promanagement saw the local labor leaders as reckless and irresponsible men who would drive out the economic base of the community without any understanding of the bind the company was in between increasing production costs, made higher by wage increases, and steadily increasing foreign competition.

In this climate of crisis the Torrington area Council of Churches, of which I was chairman, invited some of the local management and labor leaders to meet with it. We found the management leaders to be responsible and community-minded men who were also aware that a company has to make a profit and that there could be no profit if they could not find a way to reduce production costs in the face of intensifying competition. They stressed their belief that labor was the key: Employees must increase man-hour productivity. They seemed open to the suggestion that increased cooperation and better communication between management and labor might help to increase plant productivity.

At the next meeting of the Social Relations Committee the labor leaders who met with us seemed to be just as responsible and community-minded as were the management leaders. They were well aware of and deeply concerned about the economic crisis in which Torrington found itself. They also were aware of the competitive bind in which management found itself. But, they said, it is a two-way proposition: It isn't all our fault, and it isn't all our responsibility to provide the solution. What is needed, they said, is more cooperation and better communication between labor and management. They went on to say that they longed for the opportunity to discuss all these matters man-to-man with management instead of only talking about contract terms in a crisis-and-conflict situation and—here they really surprised us—that they would be delighted if the churches would help arrange such meetings.

In the face of such an invitation to help, there was nothing else to do but try. But how? We had learned quickly from the candid leaders of the two camps that one way *not* to help was the way the clergymen had chosen: to stand on the side lines and, from what seemed to others to be a superior moral stance, to offer moralistic advice about responsibility and sweet reasonableness. One of the labor leaders told us that when he read the clergymen's statement in the newspaper, he realized that these men did not have the slightest idea of what was going on, and yet they felt free to offer moral advice! What the clergymen should realize, the labor leader went on, was that every man on that negotiating committee felt that the clergymen had pulled the rug out from under them. The net result of the clergymen's appeal was to increase the anger of the negotiators and thus unwittingly intensify the conflict.

That kind of helpfulness was out. But what was in? First, we recognized that a group that could help labor and management to get together would have to respresent the entire religious community. So, we invited the Roman Catholics and the Jewish community to join us in an interfaith commission. As it finally turned out, we had on the commission one minister and one layman from the Protestant community, a priest and a layman from the Catholic community, and the rabbi from the Jewish community, with me as chairman.

My most vivid memory of the first meeting of the Interfaith Commission is how scared everyone was. We agreed unanimously and quickly that (1) we were involved in something that was of absolutely vital significance to the community; (2) that something must be done; (3) that we did not know what that something was or where we should begin; (4) that we felt foolish in our ignorance and pretentious in our roles; and (5) that we were not about to sail into such a sensitive area and monumental problem until we were more knowledgeable and better prepared.

The only honest thing that can be said about the commission in the next two years is that we dawdled and doodled along under the excuse of becoming more knowledgeable. We did not become more knowledgeable; we simply wasted valuable time. By fooling around, we contributed our share to the conditions that precipitated the bitter and costly seventeen-week strike of 1963-64 in Torrington's largest industry.

The strike surprised everyone, including some management and labor leaders. The issues were not clearly drawn, and even during the strike I was told by some industrial insiders that they really did not understand what the strike was all about. Many people in the community grumbled of a "pointless strike" as the weeks wore on. But they were wrong. The issues were there—very real and very deep. They were not the easily understood economic issues, however, and they had not been formulated or articulated very well. Perhaps this was because there was no forum in which they could have been articulated and comprehended before the crisis of the strike erupted.

I say "perhaps" because I really do not know what the situation was between labor and management at that time. The commission, including myself, had been so timid that we had established no real relationships with either management or labor leaders. We were almost as much on the outside as everyone else. It is only fair to point out that all that I have written so far is from the perspective of a concerned but ignorant layman in labor-management affairs and may be, therefore, inadvertently distorted or inaccurate.

As the strike wore along through the early winter of 1963, a great number of organizations and individuals made available their good offices to help settle the strike. The few persons who knew of the existence of the Interfaith Commission suggested that we join the ranks of the good intentioned. We resisted the suggestions because we felt that since we were too ignorant and ineffectual to help prevent the strike, we were certainly in no position to help settle it. Shortly before the strike was settled, however, I spoke to the federal mediator who had been working with the parties in the dispute and told him that I simply wanted him to know of the commission's existence. He replied that he was grateful to hear that we were not offering to settle the strike. With some feeling he stated that it seemed to him that nobody was willing to make the effort to help prevent a strike, but everyone was quite willing to settle one! He told me quite bluntly that we had no right to enter the picture now. "You had your chance to help once, but you dropped the ball. But," he went on, "someday the strike will end, and then you will have your chance to help." He assured me that there *was* a useful role for the commission and that we should press with vigor for a relevant place in the local labor-management scene.

By the time the strike was settled in February of 1964, every commission member knew that now was the time to begin to act. No matter how ignorant and inexpert we were, we had to move. In fact, perhaps our very ignorance could be used to effect. At least no one could accuse us of trying to settle the issues for them when we did not even know what they were!

The first real step toward effectiveness was taken on the day that we met with a member of the Connecticut State Labor Relations Board and heard him suggest that we try the educational approach. He told us to avoid trying to get labor and management leaders together to discuss the issues that divide them, for they will not risk weakening their bargaining position in such meetings. Nevertheless, they might respond to a joint educational venture in which outside professionals would provide general background information and where purely local and divisive issues were not raised. Did he know of any such programs already in existence, and did he know whether the University of Connecticut, through its Torrington branch, might be willing to get involved in such a venture? Our advisor gave a negative answer to both queries.

So, we had a good idea (or at least it seemed like a sensible one to the commission) but no help, no guidelines, no previous experience to go on. Finally, realizing that all anyone could do to us was to say "No," it was decided to approach the University of Connecticut, through the Torrington branch director. The university had never heard of such an idea as we proposed but was willing to give it a try. The university School of Business Administration and its Labor Education Center agreed to cooperate in the program, if we could work out a manageable format for it.

Several months and many meetings later we had progressed to the point at which we could present to both parties a prospectus for a proposed course of study for management and labor leaders of the Torrington area.

We now had a product all neatly developed and packaged, but did we have a market; would anyone buy it? We had not the slightest idea. We had decided that the commission would make no approach to either labor or management until we had a definite concrete proposal to present. With this approach, if they turned down our proposal, we could ask for a counter proposal and thus establish a relationship that dealt always with a concrete situation. Above all else we were afraid of being seen as meddling do-gooders who had nothing more to offer

37

than generalities and appeals to vague principles. Now we had what we considered a serious and sound proposal, and we were ready to see if we had a market.

We approached the Greater Torrington Labor Council, which is composed of representatives of all the local unions, and a group of leaders in industrial personnel management. Both groups were receptive to our overtures but with a certain reserve. Neither party was about to buy a pig in a poke!

We got the impression from both groups that there was an awareness of the need for an instrument or agency that would encourage better relations between them. There was never on either side any polemics against the other, but there did seem to be suspicion.

The discussions moved, it seemed to us, very slowly and deliberately. I became increasingly aware of how vital is the word "communication" and yet how difficult! A term that seemed crystal clear to some would have a whole different range of implications for others, and so time would have to be taken to find out what it meant for all concerned. We were to discover later that we could have used even more time in clarifying what was said and meant, for we found ourselves involved in situations in which the whole program was placed in jeopardy by misunderstanding.

Finally, in October of 1965, we thought we understood one another well enough to schedule the first course. It was decided to have an eight-session course which would meet for three hours each Monday evening in the facilities of the Torrington branch of the University of Connecticut. Twenty-eight labor leaders and an equal number of management leaders were enrolled, with the expenses being met by the plants and unions represented. The cost was fifty dollars per person.

The course was set up so that each participant would take two classes each evening, one on labor and one on management. Between the two class periods there was a half-hour coffee break which allowed the participants to relax and learn to know one another better.

With so many different organizations and individuals involved in setting policy and making decisions, there were, naturally, many differences of opinion, misunderstandings, tensions, and cross purposes. Most often the cause was rooted in that one word, "communication." The course became a laboratory for commission members in which they dealt firsthand with some of the basic factors that complicate the relationship between labor and management.

Midway through the initial course we had each participant fill out an evaluation sheet. The response revealed that almost one hundred percent of the labor and management leaders believed that the course was helpful and that there should be a continuing program for improving labor-management relations.

When the course ended just before Christmas 1965, all the six agencies involved agreed that the endeavor could be called a success. The participants had derived some values from it and wanted to continue the program. There had been weaknesses, and obviously there were whole areas of concern to labor and management that had not been adequately dealt with. All agreed, however, that it was a good beginning.

In January, 1966, the commission met with the coordinating committee (composed of three labor leaders and three personnel management leaders) and representatives of the University of Connecticut. It was agreed that the commission and the coordinating committee should do more work on the objectives of the continuing program before any further discussion with the university.

The two groups met in late January and discussed the objectives for the continuation of the program. They agreed that the next step was to find out from responsible persons in both labor and management just what they saw the present labor-management situation in Torrington to be, to discover what areas needed to be improved and what type of continuing program would be most helpful.

A group, composed of about twenty labor and management leaders, plus the six coordinating committee members, has met several times with the commission.

There is general agreement among group members that the most important thing that can be done right now to improve labor-managment relations in Torrington is to develop better channels of continuing communication between the two groups. One idea that was discussed extensively was that of an "open-door" policy in each local plant—the policy of easy access to one another and of person-to-person communication in addition to (and hopefully before) the contract made in the formal grievance, arbitration, and negotiating procedures.

Person-to-person communication was stressed as of number one importance. Especially was the value of this seen in interpreting contract contents. The group was unanimous in agreeing that the noneconomic factors were as important as the economic factors. Personal relationships, human values, and dignity were of greatest importance.

Another suggestion that received unanimous support was that a continuing, informal labor-management discussion group be established and maintained in each plant.

It was decided that a carefully prepared "white paper" setting forth the findings and recommendations of this joint group should be sent to every local plant and union, with special emphasis on the value of the "open-door" policy and the continuing labor-management discussion group in each local plant.

As of this writing, we have not discussed what, if any, course we will schedule next under the auspices of the University of Connecticut. There is no clear consensus in the group of the value of this more formal educational approach using university personnel. Perhaps because I am an ex-schoolteacher, I would like to see continue some type of community-wide formal education. Particularly do I believe that casework type seminars and weekend retreats under professional supervision would be of great value. These are my own sentiments, however, and I cannot speak for the group or predict how it will act to meet its own needs.

I think it is safe to say that both the labor and management leaders are firmly committed to some type of continuing program of mutual education and cooperation. What form it will take remains to be seen, but that it will take shape we have every reason to be confident. It is also safe to say that both labor and management already see very clear evidence of the value of this type of program. Both groups of leaders have said to others in my presence that they already see some signs of an improved climate in labor-management relations, and there has been no hint from any of them that they intend anything else than to work for an even more effective, mutual program.

Finally, and perhaps most importantly, it has been a source of joy to me—and I am sure to every other person who has participated in this experiment in industrial reconciliation—to see the labor and management leaders learning to like one another and to enjoy working on a joint project of value to them all. They are to one another no longer "labor leaders" or "management men," but Bill and Grace and Tom and Russ and Bernie and Ange.

Perhaps this bit of conversation I happened to overhear between the personnel manager and the chief union negotiator of one of the local industries will indicate what is beginning to happen in labor-management relations in the Torrington area. The labor leader told the personnel manager of his deep concern about the 5,500 industrial workers who have to commute to work in other communities. The personnel manager replied, "That surprises me, for we in management have always thought that you union leaders were all for people going out of town to work—that reduces the local available work force and thus enhances your bargaining position with us." The labor leader replied, "No! We don't look at it that way. Every person who goes out of town is a father or brother or son or mother or sister or daughter of one of our union people. My own son is one of them, and I know that the most dangerous place in the world for him is on the highway. They aren't something to bargain about. They're people." The manager replied softly, "Yeah! Funny! We never looked at it that way."

3

The Changing Face of a Church

Paul C. Carter, Jr.

We are a small group of people who are the remnant of the Church of St. John the Baptist. Some of us have been members of the church for a long time. We have many pleasant memories of its past, and we think of it as "our church." As long as we live reasonably close to the neighborhood, this will continue to be our church. We will support it and try to keep it as much as possible the way we have it fixed in our memory.

Some of us have been members for a shorter period of time. When we first began to attend, the Church of St. John the Baptist was similar to other churches we had joined. The Sunday worship service was a lovely experience and gave us a personal, spiritual uplift. There was a regular, graded church school for our children and an adult Bible study class for those who wanted to attend. There was a ladies' society in which one could do things for the church.

Now the Church of St. John the Baptist is changing, and we are finding it more and more difficult to keep the church the way it was. There may be many reasons why this is so, but it seems to us that behind the changes lie three important factors.

The first factor is the changing nature of our community. Many of our most active members have moved away. People who are moving into our community do not seem eager to become deeply involved in our church. As a result the membership and the budget are not as large as they used to be. We are not able to run as many church programs as we once did, and we cannot keep our building in very good condition.

The second factor which makes it more difficult to keep our church life as we are used to it is that outside financial support is diminishing. At one time the city society supplied us with funds to hire a missionary and other fulltime Christian workers. Funds to hire these workers are no longer available to us, however, and we have neither the time nor the talent to carry on in their place.

The third factor is the clergy. Of late they have been telling us that we should not focus our energy so much upon keeping a large membership, a sound building, and a smoothly running church program. It is more important, they say, to focus our attention on nonchurch affairs such as housing, education, civil rights, and world peace.

Although we would rather see the church remain the same, most of us recognize that the forces of change are too strong now for us to resist them for long. Whether we like it or not, change is coming to our church.

The first major change is taking place in our fellowship life. It was once suggested that a special committee be appointed to study biblical concepts of the church and to compare them with our own patterns of church life. From the perspective of the kind of church fellowship described in the Bible, the committee saw that there was something lacking in our traditional ways of doing things. Whereas in the life of the biblical church the close fellowship and concern of the members for one another and for all men was a demonstration of the reconciling love of God, in the Church of St. John the Baptist our fellowship amounted to little more than the clannishness of the older members, the monthly meetings of the ladies' society to plan the next dinner, and the warm but hasty greetings exchanged by those worshiping on Sunday mornings.

At the conclusion of its study the committee recommended that the church change its pattern of fellowship. Taking a clue from the example of the East Harlem Protestant Parish, the committee recommended that the church inaugurate what are now called neighborhood meetings. These are small group meetings held in members' apartments during the week for the purpose of studying next Sunday's scripture passage and relating it to our lives.

The response of the church was good from the start. We began meeting monthly, then bimonthly. Now we meet nearly every week in three different apartments and find that these meetings offer us a channel through which we can know one another on a far more intimate basis than before. Consequently, we share in one another's joys and sorrows more easily.

The discussion not only involves next Sunday's scripture passage, but also our own lives and our own communities, as we seek to find ways that the Scriptures relate to our immediate circumstances. Out of this encounter have arisen some service projects to our community. From one discussion which touched on problems of youth, we developed a Youth Job Night and invited the young people of our neighborhood into our gym for dancing and refreshments. We also invited employment agencies, schools, and other resource groups to send representatives to refer the youth to places where they could find jobs. The young people swamped us, and we expect to expand this service in the future.

Out of a neighborhood meeting, discussion which touched on problems of young children led to the development of a summer library and reading program. Discovering that in the summer there were no library facilities open to children in our neighborhood, we set aside a room in the church building as a library, moved in some bookshelves, and publicized our need for volunteers and serviceable children's books. The library, was opened two afternoons each week, and we found that there was more than enough interest among the neighborhood children to keep us quite busy.

At about the same time that the neighborhood meetings began to grow, the ladies' society meetings came to an end. We accepted the change somewhat reluctantly at first, but now we can see that the neighborhood meetings have helped to deepen our relationships with one another and our attempts to serve in the community, and have helped us gain a new and deeper appreciation of what the New Testament means by fellowship.

The second major change in our church life has been taking place in our pattern of Sunday worship. It began one Sunday morning when we were to have a baptism in our worship service. This was the pastor's first baptism in our church, and it was not until the week before that he learned how the baptistry could not be opened unless the altar were removed. The traditional arrangement of furniture had always been to keep the baptistry closed in order to have some floor space on which to put the altar. The pastor asked a question about the correctness of the symbolism in this furniture arrangement. Should the worship furniture be arranged in such a way that the baptistry must remain closed and hidden? He recommended that the church experiment with some new arrangments of worship furniture.

He and the deacons worked together and proposed a temporary but very controversial plan. The pews were placed in a horseshoe shape around the communion table to symbolize the church as a fellowship, with the pulpit moved to a central location to symbolize that the fellowship is under orders from God. Finally, the altar was removed, and the baptistry was left open to symbolize that we are under orders for mission.

Our reaction was mixed. A few of us liked it. Most of us preferred the traditional way. Some were horrified and decided then and there to withdraw membership. In the controversy that followed our biggest weakness became apparent. Some were so committed to keeping the church the same as we had always known it that they were incapable of tolerating even a temporary change in our church life. We replaced the furniture in its original arrangement sooner than we had planned in an attempt to regain the fellowship of those who left. It became apparent, however, that as far as they were concerned, irreparable damage had already been done. Those who were the most opposed to change wanted nothing more to do with us. The occasion was sad; but we lived through it.

We have discovered in our experimentation since then that changes in our worship life can be meaningful to many of us. At this moment our basic pattern of worship is as follows:

1. Recital of our church covenant
2. Presentation of our concerns and prayers
3. Proclamation of the Word
4. Confession of sin
5. Presentation of resources

Our worship begins with the reading of the church covenant. Essentially this is a declaration of our purpose as the church of Jesus Christ.

The next act is the presentation of the concerns of the church for the world. This is a time when we bring to the attention of the rest of the church the problems or opportunities about which we are concerned in our personal lives, our immediate neighborhood, our city, our nation, or our world. We write our concerns on small index cards placed in the pew racks. The ushers collect them and bring them to the communion table where the pastor reads them aloud and then structures the morning intercessory prayer around them.

At first very few of us used the cards. In fact, one Sunday

no one submitted any concerns at all. That time, instead of a prayer of intercession, we joined in a confession of sin. Soon, however, we began to get used to the idea that so-called "worldly concerns" have a very real place in worship. We began to mention our concerns for sick friends and relatives, our concerns for the city, for good elections, for good legislation, and so forth. Some of our concerns were so important to us that we even began to discuss them with one another in this section of our worship. We discussed the Civil Rights Bills of 1964 and 1965. We made decisions to send letters to our representatives, to send members to demonstrations in Washington and Selma. We heard reports from the members during this part of worship when they returned from their involvements.

We discussed the New York state bill against capital punishment, and we decided to urge our assemblyman to support it. We later made a trip to Albany to familiarize ourselves with the site of the legislative process.

At times we invited local civic leaders to speak to us on local neighborhood problems during this section of worship. As the result of one speaker and the ensuing discussion, we became somewhat involved in local housing issues.

Our third act of worship is the proclamation of the Word. Here our pastor reads and preaches on the scripture passage which we have read and studied at the neighborhood meeting the week before.

The fourth act is a unison and then silent prayer of confession which is followed by words of assurance and the Lord's Prayer.

Our final act of worship might be called the presentation of our resources. In this section the offering is collected and brought to the communion table where one of our ushers gives the prayer of dedication. The service is concluded at this point with a responsive benediction.

We are deeply sorry that changes in our worship life have cost us members. We also miss the sense of spiritual tranquillity which was present before we began discussing worldly matters in our concerns section of worship. But these changes have brought us a new understanding that true worship involves serving our neighbor, and this we appreciate. We also find it is now much more difficult to doze off during Sunday morning worship.

The third major change in our church life is the adoption of a new church covenant and constitution. Together these instruments have given us an improved method of self-government.

When we began to be involved in controversial issues, we discovered the need for a clearer definition of our purpose than the one our traditional covenant offered us. We found considerable help in the work which First Baptist Church of Chicago had done on its covenant. After several revisions we adopted a version of it which is our own.

As it stands now, our covenant is in four parts, each of which is read responsively. The first part names the participants in the covenant: God and the church. The second part describes the story of our relationship and is, in effect, a summary of the biblical story. The third section states the necessity of our free response to God through deeds of love. Two very crucial lines in this part which were debated at some length read:

Leader: Our Lord has called us to live in order to serve.

People: Therefore, we intend to arrange our church life, work, and worship in such a way that we shall be equipped for these ministries.

We also include in this section some very specific ways in which we intend to respond to God's love. These specifics change as the needs and opportunities change. At one time we were concerned that there was a lack of adequate housing in our neighborhood which is open to those of all social, economic, and racial backgrounds. Our covenant read: "We will seek to discover ways to provide better housing in this neighborhood for all people."

The fourth section states that the covenant shall be read at each worship service, that church membership shall consist of those who sign the covenant every year, and that the covenant shall be revised often according to our new insights and tasks.

In order to carry out the purpose of our covenant, it was felt that we needed more effective administrative procedures. We decided to revise our constitution making it as simple and flexible as possible. In this task we were helped by the work of the First Baptist Church of Euclid, Ohio.

The constitution affirms that the final authority in the church shall be the will of the voting membership. However, most of this authority is delegated to one central board, the church council, which has the task of providing for the implementation of the church covenant and which has the power to act on behalf of the church.

The new covenant does not sound as beautiful as the old one, and the membership requirements of our new constitution are stiffer than some of us would like. Nevertheless, we find that the covenant is helping us to gain a clearer idea of what the church is for, and the new constitution makes running the church much less complicated.

We have learned to live with these three major changes; we have even learned to appreciate and enjoy them. We regret, however, that some familiar patterns are gone and the new patterns have not made our church grow in membership size or in finance. In fact, if anything, these changes have resulted in a smaller membership and reduced finances. This means that in the future we shall be able to carry on even fewer traditional church activities, and thus even more changes will have to be made.

At the moment we are concerned that we will no longer be able to afford a fulltime pastor. This has raised some rather disturbing questions for us. How can the Word of God be proclaimed without a professional preacher to stand behind the pulpit? How will the church's ministries be carried out without a professional minister to do them? What will happen to the church without a professional administrator to keep the wheels turning?

We are distressed by these questions, and we regret that they have to be asked. However, whether we like it or not, we now must seek answers to them. We suspect that the answers will involve changes far greater than any that the Church of St. John the Baptist has yet experienced.

4

We Have This Ministry

Charles W. Gelbach

The charge was simple, or so it seemed: "Spend one year studying the concept of youth ministry and what it means for our church and community—then report back to us." This was the charge read to an ad hoc committee authorized by the Christian Education Committee of the church.

All had not been going well in the senior-high youth program. The traditional Sunday evening Pilgrim Fellowship had been combined with the senior-high church school class into a Saturday morning fellowship which included fellowship, recreation, several discussion groups, folk singing, and drama. On Sunday morning many in this group ushered, helped in church school classes, sang in the Youth Choir, or attended worship services with their families. For several years this approach worked well. Then the pressures of more and more young people working on Saturdays, family activities, and school events began to take an ever-increasing toll. The time seemed right to strike out in new bold directions. The question was, however, what directions and why. An already hard working Christian Education Committee had no time to spend long hours seeking the answers to these questions; thus, the decision was made to establish a Youth Ministry Advisory Committee to study the concept of youth ministry, evaluate the existing youth programs, and to recommend the directions for the future.

The selection and recruitment of persons for the Youth Ministry Advisory Committee (or YMAC) were deliberate and manipulated. The Christian Education Committee decided that the composition of the YMAC should include an equal number of young people and adults, and equal number of males and females, and an equal number of those presently involved in youth programs and those not involved. As persons were contacted and asked to serve on the committee, they were definitely told that if they accepted, they could expect to spend many long hours in meetings and many hours doing homework.

The twelve were finally chosen: three high-school girls, three high-school boys, two housewives, two school teachers, a corporation accountant, and an insurance agent. Some were members of the youth group; some were not. Several were advisors to the youth group, and some were on the Christian Education Committee. All shared a common interest in the future of the church's ministry to and with the youth of the church and community.

However, the appointment of twelve persons to a committee does not instantaneously produce a working group even if they share a common concern. Many on the committee knew one another only by face, but a few knew one another well enough to be perfectly honest in discussions and such. The bringing together of persons representing several different generations posed yet another problem. The first task, obviously, was to provide some way for these twelve persons to learn to know one another and to accept others as persons each with equal rights and responsibilities on the committee regardless of age, status, or occupation.

Outside, the wind was cold, but inside it was warm and cozy as the twelve gathered around the fireplace of a nearby retreat center for a weekend of just getting to know everyone and beginning to acquaint themselves with their appointed task. With them were their retreat leaders, namely, the associate minister of their own church and the associate minister of Christian education of the state conference. The senior-high young people had gathered at one side of the fireplace, and the adults were on the other side. The retreat was opened with an audio-visual presentation which had been prepared by the state conference Christian Education Department. The central theme of the presentation was nurture, stressing particularly the importance of interpersonal relationships. The painful silence that followed the presentation was indicative of the distance felt between one another. The masks had to be taken off if these twelve persons were to become a working group.

Large sheets of paper, felt-tip pens, crayons, glue, and magazines were scattered around the floor. Each teen-ager was asked to prepare a composite picture of adults and each adult was asked to prepare a composite picture of teen-agers. The results were very revealing. The teen-agers generally viewed adults as nice people, big wheels, stone faces, bosses, and very much wrapped up in their own affairs. One picture still remains very much engraved on the minds of the entire committee. An eighth-grader had prepared a simple but profound picture. In one corner of the picture was a small cartoon bearing the caption, "They never know what is going on." The major portion of the picture was a drawing of a cardtable with cards, drinks, and cigarettes all laid out in order and bearing the caption, "Why are parents never home on Saturday nights?" Adults generally portrayed teen-agers as carefree, interested in having fun, getting an education, and acquiring the "good" things in life. The walls of the room were slowly covered as each presented and explained his picture.

When this was completed, each person then prepared a second picture—a picture of himself. The results were even more revealing. Life goals, day-to-day pressures, concerns for problems of community, nation, and world, the search for self-understanding, the search for faith, the need for vital interpersonal relationships vary little regardless of age. The uniqueness of each person was quite evident, but more important the revealed alikeness that all shared provided the foundation for all to respect and accept one another as persons. Barriers of age, occupation, status, and sex dropped away. Perhaps one teen-ager summed it up when she remarked, "I never knew adults were like this!" That evening the group scattered around the fireplace, in the library, in other parts of the house, all the while sharing the insights each had received that day. A new spirit was very much present—a spirit of oneness. The same spirit was present the next morning as the group gathered around the dinner table for a celebration of the Lord's Supper. On the table was a loaf of bread and a pitcher of grape juice. Youth and adults sat interspersed around the table. The elements were consecrated, and then each was passed around the table with each person serving the person seated beside him. As the group traveled home, all realized that something exciting and profound had happened. Each one had discovered the others as persons. All were convinced that this was a key to a vital ministry of the church to and with young people and with all people.

Progress had been accomplished, but the struggle was far from over. Meeting at least monthly and often two and three times a month, the group continued to wrestle with its appointed task. The most valuable resources proved to be *Youth Ministry Manual* by Robert D. Dewey and published by the United Church Press; *Focus,* a small magazine published by the United Church of Christ; and *Folio 1964,* issued by the Department of Youth Work of the National Council of Churches. The nature of the church and ministry was the subject of numerous discussions. Finally, some decisions were made. *A Platform for Youth Work* by Virginia L. Harbour,[1] editor of youth publications, National Council of the Protestant Episcopal

[1] See *International Journal of Religious Education,* March, 1964.

Church, was adopted as the recommended basis of any future youth work in the church. The platform stresses both the necessity of continual deepening of each person's awareness and knowledge of the historic faith while at the same time stresses the need for very significant interpersonal relationships between adults and youth. Ministry, as defined by the committee, is that unique function of each Christian person who wishes to develop more fully as a Christian, which consists of learning, sharing, and living those truths and joys each has found in being a part of the fellowship of Christ's people. It means learning to be a servant and also being one unto all people today even as Christ was a servant unto all people in his day. The goals were agreed upon. The church's ministry to and with youth consisted of both ministering to their needs and helping them to prepare and minister to the needs of others.

Idealistic? Yes! Theologically sound? Yes! Practical? Perhaps! Possible to translate into programs? This was the next question to be answered. The struggle continued, and slowly a plan of action began to take shape.

The center of the program was named the Senior-High Youth Forum. This organization would have as its membership all the senior-high young people of the church and all others who would wish to take part in the program. The group would meet monthly—Sunday afternoons for three hours for worship, program, and dinner. Radiating out from the Youth Forum like spokes from the hub of a wheel would be sixteen program opportunities for members of the Youth Forum. These program groups would include (1) the Saturday Seminar—a Saturday morning study group which would let the world set its curriculum and agenda; (2) the Tube Watchers—a group which would meet to watch and/or discuss programs presented on television; (3) the Youth Choir; (4) the Chancel Players—a performing drama group which would prepare one-act plays or major productions for presentation in the church; (5) the

Church School Workers; (6) Youth Travels—a group which would study and travel to places of interest such as areas of Christian concern and renewal, churches of different denominations, new and/or unusual churches, etc.; (7) the new Christian Minstrels—a group for those interested in folk singing and folk music; (8) Teen Night Committee—a group to make arrangements for a monthly community teen dance; (9) Special Service Corps—a group for those interested in doing volunteer work in nursing homes, hospitals, and public service agencies; (10) Youth Asks—short-term study groups, eight weeks in length, using any title in this series published by Thomas Nelson and Sons; (11) Christian Encounters—short-term study groups, eight weeks in length using any title in this series published by Concordia Publishing Company; (12) the Theater Guild—this group would read and attend selected plays and movies using as guidelines the materials published in the *Green Sheet* and the *Mass Media Ministries Newsletter;* (13) the Muscle Users—a work group recruited from the Youth Forum for special projects; (14) the Forum Facts Staff—a group to prepare a monthly youth newsletter; (15) the Youth Ushers —a group responsible for the ushering in the sanctuary; and (16) the Coffeehouse Committee—a group responsible for the development and operation of a teen-age coffeehouse.

When the Youth Ministry Committee had finished working out detailed descriptions of this program, a preliminary report was presented to the Christian Education Committee. Enthusiastically the Christian Education Committee authorized the Youth Ministry Advisory Committee to continue its research and planning and to make plans for the implementation of its recommendations. The only reservation expressed was whether or not sufficient adult support could be found to operate the proposed programs. Confident that all obstacles could be overcome, the Youth Ministry Advisory Committee continued its task. Membership lists of the church were gleaned for possible leadership persons. The committee members, going out two by two, began a visitation program aimed at enlistment of adult support for any of the proposed programs if they were implemented. The response was overwhelming; over ninety percent of adults visited fully endorsed the proposed programs and offered their services in any way needed. The YMAC was now ready to submit its final report to the Christian Education Committee—nine months after it had begun its work.

The report contained the following recommendations: (1) the establishment of a permanent Youth Ministry Committee, composed of six young people and six adults, responsible for the implementation of the YMAC's recommendations and for continual administration and evaluation of the total program; (2) the adoption of the platform for youth work and the goals and definitions agreed upon by the YMAC as the basis for all future youth ministry in the church; (3) the establishment of a representative Student Council including the usual officers with responsibility for the conduct of the Youth Forum meetings and the programs emanating from them; (4) immediate introduction and implementation of the program recommendations.

These recommendations were thoroughly studied by the Christian Education Committee and then enthusiastically approved. The members of the Advisory Committee were asked to serve for one year as the permanent Youth Ministry Committee and to complete plans for the introduction of the program to the young people of the church.

The first meeting of the Youth Forum was planned as an introduction to the total program. Personal invitations were sent to every senior-high young person connected in any way with the church. About fifty percent replied that they would attend. Their reasons for accepting the invitation were obviously varied—a free dinner, curiosity, genuine interest, and so forth. Whatever their reasons, the young people came and heard and discussed the plan for youth ministry as adopted by the Christian Education Committee. The response was again enthusiastic for the program in general, though some parts such as the coffeehouse, youth travels, teen night, and several other groups were very popular. Nevertheless, registrations and information forms filled out by those attending this meeting gave a mandate to the Youth Ministry Committee to set in motion the total program just as soon as humanly possible.

Just a few months have passed since that first Youth Forum meeting; however, many exciting things are happening. The Youth Travels group has now fifteen youth members and five adult members. Their first trip took them to the worship services in a synagogue in a nearby city. Plans are now being completed for their second trip—this time to several churches in New York City. Adults have volunteered not only their time and talents but also the use of their cars.

The Special Service Corps under the guidance of a registered nurse and several other interested adults has a membership of fifteen young people. Contacts with medical and mental hospitals and public service agencies have been established, and schedules are being arranged for the placement of the young people in volunteer positions. Meetings of the group are held to discuss experiences and reasons for being involved in volunteer work.

An outstanding lawyer is now leading a small group of boys in a discussion of politics and government. The Saturday Seminar, another small group, is presently discussing the subjects of man in a technological society. The Youth Ushers, the Youth Choir, and the Church School Helpers continue functioning since they were already existing as groups, but these groups are incorporated now into the total plan for youth ministry. Another study group entitled Youth Considers Sex has begun meeting recently, again under the leadership of several very capable adults. Plans are being drawn up by another group anticipating the opening of a coffeehouse in one of the church buildings. Preparations for this has included attendance at a consultation on the coffeehouse movement and the visitation of several coffeehouses in nearby cities.

The Forum Facts Committee, under the leadership of a former assistant editor of a local newspaper, is putting out a monthly dittoed newsletter entitled "Forum Facts." Communication is an absolutely vital part of the total program. The Student Council has been elected and has started consideration of its duties and responsibilities. The Youth Ministry Committee has conducted several leadership seminars in order to help adults prepare to lead groups now in the planning stages. Recent Youth Forum meetings have had as programs a showing of the film, "The Bridge," with a discussion of the Christian and war and a discussion of "Parents as People," led by a psychologist and director of a family counseling service.

What the future holds is not completely certain. Goals have been established: (1) to help each person accept, prepare for, and carry out his own ministry; (2) to provide significant encounters of adults and youth; and (3) to make possible a vital confrontation of the historic faith with the contemporary world. The youth ministry of our church will always be directed toward the needs of individuals and not primarily toward programs. Nevertheless, high quality programs will always be a part of our youth ministry. We have examined the need of our youth in our community, the concept of youth ministry, and our previous programs. This study resulted in the programs described. Perhaps this process will enable other churches to identify their ministry to and with the youth of their church and community. Nothing risked is certainly nothing gained. Mistakes have been made, but also some victories have been won and a youth ministry discovered.

5

Ekklesia

C. Loren Graham

Each Sunday morning at about nine o'clock, a little church that might be called a big family meets in a home or in a room provided by a divinity school. No one watches the clock, for time seems unimportant. Everyone waits for the nature of the service to unfold because each Sunday service is likely to be new and unique. The emphasis is on originality and relevance. Everyone will take part, and there will be a spirit of acceptance of everyone, young or old. Any visitor will be treated as one of the group, whether he be a visiting minister satisfying his curiosity or a former prisoner on parole who may have been invited by one of the members.

Before the morning topic is announced, there is a time of sharing when each person has an opportunity to relate some happening of the past week or some insight which seems significant to him. This might be an idea that came during prayer or meditation, or an important meeting attended, a clipping from a newspaper, a page from a book, or a word about a person who is ill or needs the prayers of the group. Usually these items are of a religious nature, but if a three-year-old tells something about her doll, or an eight-year-old tells of a triumph at school, everyone understands, for children have difficulty distinguishing the secular from the sacred, and the adults in Ekklesia believe that perhaps too much distinction has been made in the past.

The worship service often begins with conventional liturgy in the form of a call to worship, a hymn, scripture reading or prayer, depending on whether these fit the objective of the leader. Responsibilities for the Sunday services are rotated among the families, and each prepares two or more consecutive services. Teen-agers sometimes prepare and lead the service, either individually or in groups. By common agreement there is no preaching or teaching in their usual forms. Preaching, the group believes, has been demonstrated to be of limited value in promoting personal involvement. Teaching, in its usual form, is unattractive to teen-agers and implies that someone already has the answers. Ekklesia avoids pat answers. The answers to modern problems can doubtless be found in the Christian heritage but are likely to require extensive study. The answers, when they have been discovered, are likely to seem genuine only to those who take part in the search; thus, personal involvement is paramount. A scripture lesson is read, often by one of the youngest children. Comments on the background of the scripture and explanations of unfamiliar terms are made by the leader. Then the leader poses one or more questions for discussion and seeks direct applications of the scripture to specific up-to-date problems. Personal problems encountered in family, school, neighborhood, and business are the type most often studied. Some leaders announce the scripture a week or more ahead to allow time for preparation.

In order to provide for the active involvement of each person, the little congregation breaks up into still smaller groups of two to six persons for discussion. No separation by ages is made, except for those under ten years. The youngsters ten or twelve years old take part in the discussion with the adults and are respected for their ideas. Children as young as eight have enjoyed discussions with one adult. It has become evident that when an adult is willing to surrender his position of "knowing it all" and listen to a child, he may gain a new insight that would otherwise have been denied him. All members of Ekklesia have made important contributions to the spiritual growth of all others.

There is no time limit set for the small group discussion. The object of the discussion is not to "teach the lesson" but to permit each person in the group to have a significant relationship with each of the others in a search for deeper meaning and value in the Christian way of life. The spiritual growth of each individual is the most important thing. The discussion is a success if each takes part in an atmosphere of sincerity, concern, and love.

On a signal from the leader the congregation reassembles for evaluation. Each small group usually makes a report, which may consist of a single insight or may be a summary of the entire discussion. This sometimes begins a whole new round of discussion by the larger group. The leader may conclude with a summary statement, or he may simply let the matter rest in the knowledge that the real results of the discussion cannot be put into words but will appear in the lives of those who took part.

On another Sunday the service might take a very different form. The group might meet in a home or have breakfast together in the park, followed by discussion around picnic tables. Sometimes the group attends a larger church. Sometimes the group meets for a common meal of New Testament simplicity, consisting of bread, soup, and fruit. This has been popular with teen-agers.

At least once a year the group spends a weekend together in rented cottages at a state park. On such occasions many friends are invited, perhaps doubling the size of the group. The program is casual and unstructured but usually results in discussions and witnessing in depth. The objective is to experience Christian relationships in a natural and happy environment as a part of everyday living, rather than a thing apart such as might be the case in a formal worship service. Sometimes the facilities have been rented for a week so that the relationships could be prolonged for all who could stay.

Ekklesia was formed in October, 1962, when four families from two large churches decided to form a small, independent group for the purpose of becoming a redemptive fellowship. No one knew at that time exactly what constituted a redemptive fellowship, and none of them would claim to know yet, but certain characteristics were agreed upon. Its purpose would be to help the world become more aware of God's love by the example of man's love for man. It would emphasize that the mission of the church is to the world and not to the nurturing of a church organization. It would emphasize personal discipline and commitment for mission and it would de-emphasize structured organization and activity for activity's sake. Emphasizing the responsibility of laymen and discouraging the tendency to shift all spiritual responsibility onto the professional clergy, it would encourage the active search for the truth on each person's part and would accept the changing beliefs that accompany spiritual growth. It would not encourage the fixation of creed or any other form of stabilization that might inhibit spiritual growth. It would not pretend to have the answers but would never fail to seek them diligently. Any organization the fellowship might form would not need to be permanent or successful as long as it was obedient to the Holy Spirit. In all its endeavors for God it would expect to find joy but not comfort or ease.

Within a few weeks after the group was formed it had become apparent that the above purposes were being interpreted as a threat to the churches. It may have been the experimental nature of the group or perhaps the implied criticism of the church organization. In any case, each of the families soon felt impelled to withdraw from their respective churches. (This

64

no longer seems to be important. Some families now associated with Ekklesia are members of other churches.)

The group felt the need of a basic church organization and about six months later was incorporated as an independent church. Each one of the original adults is a trustee (to meet legal requirements), but the church has no other officers or leaders and no pastor. It does not have any formal membership. It is believed that membership should not be casual or easy but should represent some significant degree of commitment and some definite spiritual growth, such as the membership requirements of the Church of the Saviour in Washington, D.C. Exactly what these should be for Ekklesia has not yet been determined. The informal membership which has resulted seems to meet the needs for the present.

Ekklesia has since formed a second corporation known as Ekklesia Foundation for the purpose of handling the real estate and business affairs required of any of the Ekklesia missions. It is the intention that each member will be "on mission"—that is, he will be engaged in some volunteer activities in which he will attempt to carry the spirit of Christ into the world. The missions have taken various forms: sponsorship of parolees and youthful offenders, case aid work in the city slums, volunteer work at the state hospital, tutoring children behind in school work or assisting in the training of crippled children, carrying a Christian spirit into the affairs of the school board. One family heads up an area Camp Farthest Out (an interdenominational religious organization), and another heads up the sponsoring committee of the Lay School of Theology at the Colgate Rochester Divinity School.

Ekklesia contributes to the favorite missions of individuals away from Rochester also. These have included several scholarships for refugee children in Hong Kong, several Negroes in New York, the South, East Harlem Protestant Parish, and so forth.

The group is seeking corporate mission in which all can take part. So far, only one approximates the requirements. One Ekklesia family sponsors a large Negro family which was having great difficulty renting a home because of fourteen children. Ekklesia Foundation was formed in order to buy a house to rent to them. A large house in good condition outside the slum area was purchased, and the family was put on the road to rehabilitation by the marked upgrading of their home condition. This was done through a voluntary agency in Rochester known as the Family Sponsorship Program. Many churches were invited to take part, and Ekklesia was the first to respond. Since then, other organizations have followed, and the program has become an experimental project of the federal government, with funds available to assist in the purchase of homes by the sponsoring organizations.

The money for these missions has not been obtained by the usual church collection. No Ekklesia meeting has ever included a collection, and no visitor has ever made a money contribution. All contributions by the members are entirely voluntary and are made quietly and individually to one designated as the business manager. The aim of the group is a tithe, but some of the members have not yet achieved this goal. However, enough money has been given so that all mission projects have been paid for immediately. The group spends very little money on itself; it owns no church buildings and has no staff. Most of the money goes into mission, except that donated to agencies such as the local council of churches and to the divinity school.

Four or five couples meet regularly one evening a week for prayer, study, discussion, and fellowship. Fellowship is believed to be at least as important as study or discussion for spiritual growth. Other adults attend when they care to. However, the meeting was restricted for a time while five couples were taking a course (thirty weeks) on human relationships, prepared by the Yokefellows. This was intended to help each participant discover the characteristics that might bear on his ability to be effective in his missions. The course was very beneficial in helping each become intimately acquainted with and adjust to all the others.

Interest in the weekly meetings has been very high, and attendance has been nearly perfect among regular members, except on occasions of illness, family emergency, or trips out of town. Discussions are informal and often unplanned, but the ideas expressed may be based upon the works of such writers as Tournier, Tillich, Thielicke, Robinson, Harvey Cox, John Casteel, Elton Trueblood, Douglas Steere, Thomas Kelly, William Stringfellow, Arnold Come, and on the recorded sermons of Gordon Cosby of the Church of the Saviour in Washington. Sometimes a lively discussion may extend well beyond midnight.

Rochester churchmen have been very curious about Ekklesia. It is surprisingly well known for such a tiny group. This may be due in part to the activity of its members in the racial and social problems of the inner city or in the activities of the local council of churches, but it is more likely that it receives attention because it is experimental in its approach to religious problems and may be considered by some to be radical.

An Ekklesia communion service might contribute to this belief. Each service has been different, and none has been like those usually found in larger churches. Some have emphasized the risen Jesus, rather than the crucified Christ. The occasion is one of joy in the fellowship with Christ, as is believed was often the case in the early church. The group sits together at a large table. Fruit juice is served in large glasses and bread in large pieces. Happy conversation is encouraged, but an awareness of the presence of the spirit of Jesus is maintained. On other occasions the group may choose to emphasize the crucifixion and atonement, and the spirit is one of confession and repentance, followed by an acceptance of grace and forgiveness.

Ekklesia people may pray with open eyes. It is believed that Jesus prayed in such a manner, probably standing with arms outstretched. God does not require a formally worded prayer but looks beyond words into the hearts of men. A thought which somehow cannot be put into words may be more eloquent than any that can be found in a prayer book. In some Ekklesia prayer services each person may in turn suggest things to pray about, but no one actually puts the prayer into words.

A special type of service is held at Christmas time, when each person prepares a gift for the group. This may be anything within the scope of a person's talent: a written prayer, a poem, a musical number, a meditation or story, a piece of handicraft, or anything that expresses an insight and says "thank you" for a meaningful fellowship.

In preparing for this article the author interviewed the twelve persons who had been associated with Ekklesia for the longest time. These included seven adults and five young people, ranging in age from twelve to seventeen. Each answered a list of twenty-four questions and then made a statement expressing beliefs, attitudes, and feelings toward the group. The interviews ranged in time from a half-hour to over two hours. Most of the group have found the Ekklesia experience very helpful, and nine of the twelve agreed that if they could belong to only one social or religious organization that it would be Ekklesia. Most have felt that significant changes have taken place in their lives. In addition to an increased understanding of Christian principles, much help has been provided in the solving of family problems, in applying Christian ethics in business, in using love and understanding in dealing with employees and fellow workers, in appreciation of the beauty of God's creation and the great worth of persons. Perhaps the most articulate response came from a seventeen-year-old girl who pointed out that the experience has caused her to mature intellectually and spiritually faster than her friends. She is accustomed to adult discussions. She was recently one of the winners in a summer foreign student exchange and attributed her being chosen to the fact that she was more easily able to establish rapport with the adults of the examining board.

She also points out that although the Sunday services seem to be extremely free and unstructured, they are actually very disciplined. Everyone must seriously attempt the solution of real life problems in a mature manner and within the Christian framework. Everyone is expected to make significant contributions. This situation is much more disciplined than most of the other situations she has experienced.

Each individual feels that the experience of the past three years has been an adventure that has made life more significant and has promoted the spiritual growth of all who have taken part. At the same time, it has been an exciting and often joyful experience. There is no reason for complacency, however; accomplishments have been trivial compared with the dreams of its members. Ekklesia is full of flaws and disappointments. Everyone is far from satisfied with his personal discipline or his commitment. All agree that the fellowship has been fun, but most of the purpose and discipline lies ahead.

On several occasions there has been an attempt to establish a written purpose and discipline that would express the intentions and goals of all the members. This has been only partially successful because the commitments have been individual and changing. The following is the most recent attempt. It expresses a common purpose, but encourages individual discipline.

We believe that separation from God and separation from others causes all the anxiety and the feelings of being unfulfilled that exist in our lives. Through the spirit of Jesus Christ, we believe the power is available to change all things in our lives. Because we want to be whole persons and with unified personalities, and be-

cause we believe in the necessity of living within redemptive communities, we will with every opportunity seek and endeavor to
change our lives through increasing our spiritual relationships with
God and through developing more meaningful relationships with
others. From day to day and moment to moment we will try for less
denial of his presence in our thinking, in our actions, in our
reflections, and in our prayers.

To the best of our abilities we will give with joy and thankfulness
of our time, talents, and treasure, and will discipline our time and
energies in favor of the deepest concerns of our lives and the lives
of others. Because we believe that much of our salvation is in the
giving of ourselves to others, we will make consistent efforts to
meet everyone in a spirit of love, understanding, and acceptance;
ever maintaining the hope of bringing compassion and strength for
new life to those suffering from pain, poverty, or ignorance; and yet
remembering that we are responsible for the ways in which we
affect others.

We will be conscious of our needs for intellectual growth, more
maturity, and a sound understanding of the faith that is within, by
increasing our familiarity with the wisdom and the insights recorded
by authors, artists, and prophets.

Because we believe that every human being has the right to live
in an environment that aids personal growth, we will try to be
instruments of God, servants in his grace, and responsive to the
power of his spirit that can touch and renew others through us.

THEREFORE, in the Presence of God, each of us will establish,
and from day to day revise, the aspirations of our personal disciplines,
which for this moment are:

What lies ahead for Ekklesia? None pretends to know.
Definite plans are difficult to formulate without destroying the
freedom for the individual growth and independent expression
of commitment upon which the group has been built. Obedience
to the will of God is the avowed intention; the individual
pursuit of truth and meaning of life is the practice. It is

recognized that these may not always be compatible, that being the body of Christ may require some greater degree of corporate purpose and endeavor than has existed so far. Everyone realizes that the pressures of living may eventually destroy any of the high purposes that have not been carefully woven into a structure of disciplined lives and formalized organization. At the same time, all believe that a formalized church structure can become ingrown, expending all its energies on self-nurture, virtually destroying all spiritual initiative and creative mission to the world. The future of Ekklesia, if it is to have a meaningful future, probably lies somewhere between the two extremes. It must not promote individualism to the extent that its members do not hear the Word of God; it must not allow corporate purpose to supplant individual commitment and creativity.

Ekklesia does not expect to grow rapidly. It is not likely to be a popular movement. There are many churches already furnishing a satisfying environment for those who wish to avoid discipline and commitment. To date, Ekklesia has made no attempt to enlarge itself; no one has been asked to join, and no one who is a member of another church has been asked to attend.

Perhaps a very significant future may emerge if two intentions can be realized: (1) Ekklesia would like to provide fellowship and love, without regard for social status, racial origin, or previous respectability for any who need help from a Christian group; (2) Ekklesia would like to provide a searching and sharing fellowship for those who see in Christianity an exciting adventure in commitment, discipline, and love but who have been unable to find such a fellowship in other existing organizations.

6

The Ministry of Bethany

John C. Garvin

Joe Hudson looked into the mirror of the men's room adjacent to his ward at Allegheny General Hospital. As he shaved, he thought of the sickening sameness of another day, of his helplessness and inability to provide for his wife and their four small children in their apartment in Northview Heights, the low-income public housing project up on the hill.

How much longer was this kind of living going to go on? It seemed as if bad luck followed that face in the mirror.

This was Joe's second trip to the hospital in a year. This seemed to be the pattern life had followed since his marriage to Sally six years ago last month. The fact of a police record earned during his late teens and early twenties, and that he had not finished high school did not help matters any. Last year, just after starting a new job as a truck driver, he had to go into the hospital for surgery to remove a cyst on his lower spine. Then, after months of unemployment again, he finally got a job with a wrecking crew, tearing down old buildings in a redevelopment area of the city's slums. After only three months on the job a rupture developed, and more surgery was required. Now there would be more weeks and perhaps months of unemployment ahead.

Joe wondered how Sally was going to buy food for the weekend. The boss had promised some help, but he never showed up. How was the management office going to be paid on Monday morning, which was the deadline for the month's rent?

A couple of years ago these problems would have been overwhelming to Joe, but now, though they troubled him, he knew he did not have to face them alone, for Joe had some friends he could count on who shared his life, his concerns. Joe had become involved in the Bethany ministry when the new chaplain moved into an apartment in his building.

Through the many contacts that followed with the Reverend Leigh Jarvis, the Bethany House chaplain, and its director, the Reverend John C. Garvin, little things began to happen to Joe and his family. The Wednesday morning "kitchen meetings" with other women from the block gave Sally a chance to meet new friends, something she had found hard to do since moving from Brooklyn. She also found that other women were having many of the same problems and meeting many of the same frustrations. Being able to discuss them freely and, at the same time, finding encouragement and enlightenment from a modern translation of the New Testament helped her to find a new dimension to life, a life now that had room for the living Christ.

Through their contacts with Bethany House, Joe and Sally soon made contacts with people from outside the project who became their friends. One couple, Clara and Vern, began to meet with them weekly on Tuesday evenings with some of the neighbors for a house church. Through the friendship of Vern, a metallurgical engineer, Joe began to grow in the Christian faith. One of the group's first projects was to help Joe find employment.

Many unemployed men in the inner city have lost the will to work. Joe was no exception. Through the Pittsburgh experiment's Tuesday noon luncheon at the downtown Pittsburgh YMCA cafeteria, Joe was introduced to employed Christian laymen who meet regularly with the unemployed. Through these contacts Joe came to know many other men who shared his concern and his struggle to find a new life. The first thing they did was to encourage Joe to enter into a thirty-day prayer experiment where he would, every day for at least thirty days, as often as he thought about it, ask God, in his own words and in his own way, for the "will to work." It was only a few weeks later that Joe landed the truck-driving job.

Meanwhile, Joe and Sally became members of the Church of Our Saviour, a new congregation that has grown out of the Bethany ministry in Northview Heights and which is now pastored by the Reverend John C. Garvin. Joe is now a trustee, and Sally is an officer in the women's society of that new congregation.

Through their involvement in the church, they have made many more new friends and now, in a time of discouragement, find that they are supported by others who are concerned. They also have come to know Christ and not only trust him, but also believe that his living presence will enable them to come through the present crisis victoriously.

Just as Joe finished shaving and walked back to his bed in the ward, he found Chaplain Jarvis waiting. They talked for sometime about Joe's recuperation from the surgery and about the family and the present financial crisis. Before having a parting prayer with Joe, Chaplain Jarvis assured him that he would get to work on the problems.

Since Joe and his family were members of the Church of Our Saviour, Chaplain Jarvis informed Pastor Garvin of the immediate need for food and financial help. From the Lord's Pantry, which is kept stocked with canned goods by church members, a variety of canned foods was gathered together and quietly taken to Sally's back door along with a check for ten dollars from the Bethany House "Ministry of Kindness Fund" to buy perishables. Pastor Garvin then arranged with the housing authority to hold off on the rent collection until he could assist Sally in getting an emergency public assistance grant to hold the family over until they could arrange for compensation or unemployment checks.

Sally's pleasant smile and cheerful greeting are welcome sights as she visits Joe in the hospital. She can smile because she knows that she does not bear her burden alone. It is also a great relief to Joe to know that God loves him and his family and that the church is interested in him. Standing by his side, he knows, are friends praying for his recovery and sharing their food and financial resources, as well as their love.

This is the ministry that operates out of Bethany House, a large old house on the edge of a housing project on Pittsburgh's north side—a ministry that has as its motto, "To love the people and let the Holy Spirit lead." From the Bethany House in Northview Heights, the church extends the strong, compassionate arm of Christ to meet the social needs of the nearly one thousand low-income families in the community. By means of the Church of our Saviour, the right hand of Christian fellowship is extended to any who come to know and profess Jesus Christ as Lord and Savior. Adjacent to Bethany House now stands a newly constructed church building that serves as headquarters for the young, but growing, congregation of the Church of Our Saviour.

The major financial support for the Bethany ministry comes from the nearly one quarter of a million Methodists in the western Pennsylvania Annual Conference through its Board of Missions and from the denomination's Division of National Missions. The Bethany ministry is administered by The Methodist Church Union, the City Missionary Society of The Methodist Church in Pittsburgh. The executive secretary is Dr. Allan J. Howes. The ministry is by no means limited to Methodists. The director and pastor, the Reverend John C. Garvin, is a former United Presbyterian minister. The chaplain

was a Disciples of Christ pastor. The new interracial congregation, though Methodist, is made up of believers from many
denominational backgrounds. The staff also includes a Christian
education director, Mrs. Betty Clemens, who heads up a weekday, as well as a Sunday Christian education, program for many
of the community's nearly three thousand children and youth.

Through the Bethany mental health services a psychologist
and a psychiatrist come to Bethany House two days a week and,
thereby, provide a community mental health service which is
desperately needed.

There is also a youth worker, John Patak, who, himself
a high-school dropout, grew up on the streets of Pittsburgh's
north side. Recently, John got to know sixteen-year-old Donald,
who began frequenting the soda fountain located in the basement of Bethany House. John noted that Donald was a troubled
youth who missed a lot of school and was often in trouble
in the community. Donald told John that he had had a hearing
in Juvenile Court and was to be sent away, but the judge could
not get him into the institution to which he had committed
him. Part of John's ministry is to stand by the side of young
men like Donald in the time of a crisis.

The judge had scheduled a second hearing to reassign
Donald. This time John was by Donald's side in the courtroom.
Because of the fine cooperation that has grown up between the
Bethany ministry and the Juvenile Court, the judge let Donald
return home where he was to stay under the close supervision
of John. The following day John went to visit at his home and
was shocked to find the deplorable home life to which Donald
was subjected. There was no father in the home, and his
mother, who still had three other children at home besides
Donald, had become so discouraged and filled with despair
that she no longer cared about anything or anyone. She imposed
no discipline upon the children, rarely cooked for them, and
had little furniture (most of which could be called junk), no

television, radio, or magazines. Little wonder Donald had taken to the streets. Little wonder he never wanted to go home to a house that had no kitchen chairs and only two forks; to a bedroom that was furnished with a ragged, urine-stained mattress in the corner without sheets or covers, and where the three-legged dresser had no drawers.

In response to this crying need, the Bethany ministry moved into action. A referral was made for Donald's mother to the mental health services. Through Goodwill Industry some decent used furniture was made available. The Economic Opportunity Program's intensive caseworker was called in. Three women in a suburban church were motivated to pool their valuable trading stamps which they used to obtain some greatly needed kitchen utensils for Donald's mother.

One Sunday recently John took Donald horseback riding with some other teen-agers. The light in Donald's eyes as he got off Ginger—John's horse that he keeps near the county's south park—began to show a spark of new life. Neither Donald nor anyone in his family have become church members, and perhaps they never will. At least we now have given Donald and his family the opportunity to know that somebody cares, that the church of Jesus Christ cares, and that they are not necessarily forgotten and forsaken children of God, lost in the crowds of the city.

Loneliness seems to haunt the tenements and apartments of the inner city. Senior citizens, especially, are its victims. Mrs. Jones, a public health nurse, called Bethany House one morning to inform Mr. Garvin of one particular need that she had recently discovered in the community.

Elderly Mrs. Helen Morgan had been one of Mrs. Jones's patients for the past several weeks. Medically, Mrs. Jones and Dr. Marcus had done all they could for her; yet she was not responding. She sat for days, staring out of the window of her ninth-floor efficiency apartment. Her meager Social Security check allowed nothing for travel after the rent was paid and some groceries were bought each month. The fact was that she had no place to go or no one to visit. Neither did she have a desire to eat, except for some black coffee, a slice of brown bread, or a boiled egg once in a while. The shelf above the sink was lined with all sizes and shapes of medicine bottles, but these did not seem to help either.

Mrs. Morgan's husband passed away over nine years ago, and her only son had been killed in World War II. She thought there was a cousin or two still living, but they were in Alabama, and she had not heard from them in years. Her few friends, which included the corner butcher, had to be left behind when the churning jaws of the bulldozers tore down her rooming house in the Manchester district. Now transplanted to the housing project's high-rise building, she was alone and frightened in a strange new environment. There she sat awaiting the day when the good Lord would take her home.

To the Reverend John Garvin, her case sounded much like that of Mr. Ellis Nared, who only three years ago became involved in the Bethany ministry under similar circumstances. Today, at seventy-eight, Mr. Nared is still very much alive, both in body and spirit. In spite of his age he is one of the leading men in the building fund drive for the new Church of Our Saviour. He testifies that the Bethany ministry made the difference in his life. He has found a purpose to go on living for and has discovered that there are many who share his life and his love.

The Senior Citizens' Lounge, located in the basement of one of the high-rise buildings, a phase of the Bethany ministry program, helped to put Mr. Nared in touch with others on a daily basis where they can help one another. At the Senior Citizens' Lounge each person knows he is needed and wanted. In addition to the daily contacts the senior citizens have with each other—some of which Dan Cupid has used to bring about new family relationships—there are interesting things to do. Late each afternoon any senior citizen can get a full course meal for sixty cents because the cooking is done voluntarily by some of the women of the group on a rotating basis. Bill Moore keeps the hedges trimmed outside the building; others serve a half day each week as official hosts or hostesses. Trips are planned, and parties are held with the senior citizens doing the work and making the arrangements for themselves. A minimum of direction is given by Mr. Bruce Connell, a senior citizen volunteer, under the supervision of Mr. Garvin. What is best is that the senior citizens' program gives lonely people like Mr. Nared, and now, we hope, Mrs. Morgan, something to live for.

One of the men most instrumental in initiating the Bethany ministry nearly five years ago in Pittsburgh was the Reverend David J. Wynne. Dr. Wynne often speaks of himself as being a "broker in opportunities." This spirit has lived on in the Bethany ministry as we seek to "love the people and let the Holy Spirit lead." We daily find new opportunities for witness and service in the name of our Lord Jesus Christ. In these and many other ways the ministry of Bethany strives to be the "church creative."

7

New-Look Church in California

Janette T. Harrington

In Marin City, California, there is a church based on the premise that the Christian faith can unify people of all sorts and conditions.

Some churches never achieve integration. Some have integration thrust upon them by whirling changes in their neighborhood. A few are born integrated. One of these few is the St. Andrew United Presbyterian Church in Marin City, California. It may be a prototype of things to come.

St. Andrew serves two towns across the Golden Gate Bridge from San Francisco. The two are as unlike as a pea and a bean in the same pod. Marin City has a population that is ninety-five percent Negro. The residents live in public housing or modest homes or urban-renewal projects of award-winning contemporary design. The town is an enclave that grew up chiefly during the shipbuilding days of World War II. It persists partly because of the unavailability of Negro suburban housing elsewhere. Tam Valley, on the other side of a pyramid-shaped hill, is an ordinary white, middle-class suburb. Its California-style houses nestle on the wooded slopes leading up to Mount Tamalpais. Thanks to a ministry that includes both communities, St. Andrew is growing up interracial.

"We are in business," explains one of its two co-pastors, "To keep that pile of dirt from becoming a symbol of the barricade between people."

There is particular significance in the direction integration is taking in this church. In car-happy California it is no trick at all to get from one community to another along the freeway. White members must drive from Tam Valley to church instead of sitting back in the hope that Negro members will find their way to a church on their side of the mountain. "For the white Christian to take the initiative," says the same pastor, "for him to sit down and join forces with us indicates that he pretty actively and vigorously means what he says."

Bolstered by seminary teams from nearby San Anselmo, the church in Marin City began life as a mission to the area's Negro population. When it appeared that a church could be established, the Reverend Don Schilling, a San Francisco Seminary graduate and former settlement-house director in Sacramento, became the organizing pastor. Before long, the congregation decided to widen its ministry and called the Reverend James E. Symons to work with Mr. Schilling. Another San Francisco graduate, Symons is a former campus pastor at Warren Wilson Junior College in North Carolina.

In the usual team pastorate, duties are divided according to specialty—preaching, counseling, or Christian education. Here each man carries on a personal ministry in the place where he lives—Schilling for Marin City, Symons for Tam Valley—while he shares a pulpit.

The reaction to the new venture shows a much higher interest index, counting visitors and persons attending but not yet members, than the present membership of eighty-five Negroes and twenty whites would indicate. This is particularly noteworthy since many people of Tam Valley have an aversion to the organized church. But they have "an acute sense of the need for reconciliation between races and between people," says Symons. These are people who became sufficiently disturbed over de facto segregation in their area schools to want to help bring about an intradistrict exchange of white and Negro pupils. "They can get highly excited about an interracial church."

The hazard, the ministers note, is that people will look at St. Andrew as just another civil rights group and may even join the church on that basis. "We make it clear that our interest in integration stems from our relation to Jesus Christ. We would contend vigorously that the biblical record is on our side, that the church of Christ is an inclusive one."

From the standpoint of ministering in a mobile age, St. Andrew, which has just moved into a new building readily accessible for miles around, also paints a preview of the future, the two ministers think. It is "old-fashioned," says Symons, not to take seriously today's freeway pattern of living. People are accustomed to driving on fast-traffic highways to shop, to dine out, to go to the movies, to visit friends. They are not likely to balk at a three or four minutes' drive to church.

"Normally in new-church development, you pick a single community with growth potential. There is a little nucleus, and you meet in temporary quarters until you can build one unit, and you keep going until you have a whole plant and a good-sized congregation." According to demographic predictions, population in the Bay Area will mount to fourteen million in the next several years. Howard Robie, former church-extension man for the north coastal area, has pointed out that this means three and a half times the present number of churches. The Marin City pattern suggests a way of serving three or four communities from one plant, using a team ministry.

When this novel approach came up in presbytery, a few people objected to "overburdening" so small a church with two ministers and two manses. On the whole, however, presbytery came down firmly on the side of investing its resources in this two-pastor, one-plant ministry. The Board of National Missions put in $45,000; presbytery contributed $42,000; and the local congregation pledged a fervent $22,000, out of scant pockets.

The Schilling and Symons team ministry has to take into account the different needs and different problems of two dissimilar communities.

In Marin City, with its high Negro concentration, the work of the church is largely shaped to the needs of "people eaten up alive by the little bites life takes out of them." By all rights, the town, one of a cluster rimming the bay that includes artist-colony Sausalito, should draw residents eager for a desirable place to live close to San Francisco. Many of the houses raised on stilts against the steep hillsides have spectacular views of the bay. For a night out, the Schillings say, they dim the lights, turn on the record player, and enjoy a panorama as fine as they would see from the Top of the Mark.

But such houses, selling at four or five thousand dollars less than the going rate in nearby towns, are hard to move. One realtor offers a hundred dollar bonus to any resident who can induce a friend to move in. "People have stereotyped ideas of a Negro community," says Schilling. "They think we all carry knives and wear greasy blue jeans." Carrying lunch boxes instead, these people head for city jobs as carpenters, electricians, or plumbers; wives work out of their homes, too. Some families barely scratch along.

A ministry to people living in high-rise housing is one of the hopes for Marin City. Preschool training for youngsters is another.

Tam Valley offers a different set of frustrations. An unincorporated town with a minimum of civic supervision, it attracts the individualist who "hopes to get away from the organization and mass involvement of the city—the gray-flannel suit and all that."

Its people are like many Californians in that they want to forget everything they left behind, including church connections. They say "We're interested in learning about the church and in discussing theology and all, but we don't want to get involved." The most common charge they level is one of irrelevancy. As most people see it, the church has nothing to say to the concerns they deal with every day of their lives. It takes, says Symons, about a hundred calls to produce any real flicker of interest.

Some open-end discussions held recently in the manse underscored Tam Valley's basic wariness of the church. One lady was quite impressed by the lively contributions of a professor—until he began to open up about his deep personal faith. "I was so *shocked,*" she recalls. Another recoiled in horror when a neighbor remarked, "I believe I saw you in church last Sunday." "Not I," she exclaimed in instant rejection of such piosity.

A variety of unorthodox approaches are being tried out in Tam Valley to magnetize people who are not ordinarily interested in church. The new church building permits activities such as the play recently given in the sanctuary, musical programs, and an art exhibit held in connection with a study of Negro history. The antipoverty program and the causes of unrest such as that in Watts are discussed in an effort to probe for deeper meanings. A Wednesday-evening Lenten series held in the manse this year features discussions on the newspaper and the Bible.

The decisive point for many comes with their realization that the church is not, as they had assumed, off in its own little corner somewhere apart from the worries of the world. Typical is Mrs. Alfred (Catherine) Averill, who in "all her thousand years of Sunday school" back east had never known a church to take a positive stand on race relations. A striking-looking woman with silver hair and a youthful face who has added an adopted part-Negro, part-Mexican baby to her family of five, Catherine Averill turned away from the church at an early age because of its "hypocrisy." Young people are astute, she thinks, about detecting the failure of so-called Christians to practice what they profess. Now, impressed by St. Andrew and its ministers, she says, "You may find me in church yet."

Misgivings are not confined to the white community; the Negro community has some too. "Many people here come from the South," says James O. Quiett, a Negro church member whose son is county president of CORE. "They harbor feelings of mistrust that have built up over a number of years." But he has high hopes for St. Andrew's build-from-scratch pattern of integration. "Most people want to see integrated churches, but they don't know how to go about it. Commonly a welcome sign goes on the door—but this often happens in communities that have no Negroes around. It is hard for the minority-group person to feel welcome."

Willa Howard, a mother of four, recalls that in the churches she used to attend the services were noisy. ("I didn't like all that shouting."). She thinks understanding of people grows when persons of different races get together.

The inevitable question asked is: How can people of widely different backgrounds blend into one congregation? The two ministers have an unequivocal answer: No problem. "Frankly," says Montana-born Schilling, "My vocabulary has never been such that I could get above anybody even if I tried."

In sermons the two ministers, who preach on alternate Sundays and take turns moderating the session, talk about "problems that affect us all." But the basic common bond is a belief "in Christ as Lord. Learning how to pray, or to seek forgiveness of sins, is as real to the professional man as it is to the domestic." New forms of worship introduced emphasize relationships between man and man, as well as those between man and God. For example, at the communion service members turn to one another with the greeting, "The Lord be with you."

The two ministers began by holding weekday church school sessions in houses near the children's own homes. This pattern is now abandoned in favor of a joint Sunday morning church school. The mingling of children of different backgrounds has advantages on both sides. As one white mother says, the experience is good for her children "because growing up in a white world today is just not realistic."

"We are thrown together in a common humanity which is very real for all of us," say the ministers. When people from the two communities get together in discussion groups, "as they begin to share, to get to know one another, as white members hear Negro members tell of the dilapidated schools and other problems, they find they have a great deal in common. Our problem has been that the evenings are never long enough for us to share what we really want to."

Plans for the future of St. Andrew envisage an assortment of ideas for showing people of the community that the church has their interests at heart. Among them are a center for art, music, and drama, and an industrial school.

In several ways the church at Marin City foreshadows the coming look in new-church development. Present stipulations on use of National Missions funds encourage the establishment of new churches on an interracial basis. Says the Reverend Harold F. Fredsell, a new-church development consultant for the Board of National Missions, "More and more we need to tackle the tough situations like Marin City." Some other tough-situation new churches currently aided by National Missions include a church in the predominantly Negro Cooper Park public-housing project in Brooklyn, a shopping-center ministry in a low-income section of Topeka, and two new Spanish-speaking churches, in the Bronx and in Washington, D.C.

"We know how to start a new church in a blossoming situation," says Mr. Fredsell, "and we have to keep doing this. But if all we are doing is going into the sure things, no mission is involved."

St. Andrew is a church on the new frontier.

8

Fractured Forms

Robert W. Shaffer

Some people call it the "barn." Others refer to it as the "all-purpose room." Upon entering it, you are quietly met by clues to the life of the people who gather in this room each Sunday morning.

What you fail to see often communicates as much as what you see. What you hear, against what you expected to hear, tells you something more.

On one Sunday morning you might be met by the fresh sounds of the Folkal Trio, a three-guitar, folk-singing group, belting out the prelude to worship. Another Sunday it might be the angry words of "The Universal Soldier" or "Mississippi," banged out by Rich Savin. Or it might be the delicate sound of unaccompanied Bach by a violinist from the music department of Glassboro State College. The acoustics are so "live" that no sounds are lost. Lately it was a jazz saxophonist with the mellow, flowing sounds of "Air for G String," accompanied by the organ.

When one enters the leanly decorated room, he can readily understand why some affectionately, others with disdain, refer to it as the "barn." The room looks somewhat unfinished. Your eye catches it all very quickly: red brick lightly brushed with white on one end, off-white, plaster walls, arched ceiling beams, grey tile floors, plain windows, wooden pews, not fastened, uncushioned. Characteristic of the rest of the room, the small Estey pipe organ is completely exposed, with no "show" pipes. The simplicity, the lack of expected symbols, speaks of a people stripping down, searching for essentials, for what is meaningful to us today. Compared with buildings in which everything is where you expect to find it, communicating the feeling that the truth has been given and all that is needed is to apply it, this room gives the impression that nothing is nailed down; that more is yet to come; that what will come next is not predictable.

The people are seated in a U-shaped arrangement. The open end of the U faces one of the long side walls. In the middle of the opening stands a ten-foot table covered with an ordinary white tablecloth. At the end of the table, closest to the wall, is a small lectern, the kind often used at banquets. In the middle of the table are a chalice and a bread plate. At the other end is a simple bowl when Baptism is to be celebrated. The people face each other around and across this table. No seats are more than four or five rows away from it. The table and the seating are all on one level. There is no chancel, no platform, no choir, no vestments.

Stripped to such simple tools as seats and tables and cups and books, the room impresses one with a fresh sense of mobility. These same people could gather for the same purpose in any building. Minus those visual "Aids to Worship" which sometimes distract us with abstractions, we are enabled to see the centrality of our neighbors sitting beside us and across the table from us. Empty, the room has little meaning because its central symbol is the people gathered in it. The mood is not iconoclastic but rather open to symbols emerging or returning which express contemporary faith, the faith of these people.

On one particular morning, walking into the room, you would see and hear in the center a string quartet made up of a father and three of his teen-age children playing a Haydn sonata.

The father directs his own internationally known music camp near Glassboro.

When they are finished, the minister comes to the lectern from a seat among the people. He begins the forty-five-minute service with these words:

With deep roots and firm foundations, may you be strong to grasp, with all God's people, what is the breadth and length and height and depth of the love of Christ, and to know it, though it is beyond knowledge. So may you attain to fullness of being, the fullness of God himself.

The people respond with:

Now unto him who is able to do immeasurably more than all we can ask or conceive, by the power which is at work among us, to him be glory in the church and in Christ Jesus from generation to generation evermore! Amen. (Eph. 3:17-21 NEB.)

With so little to distract ears and eyes, the *words* that are used seem to gather intensity, seem to be greeted expectantly. Again you find yourself listening for clues.

A hymn is sung unaccompanied. The sound of your neighbors is not covered. You find yourself listening to your neighbor, feeling his presence, sensing your relationship with him.

The scripture reading is from the Gospel of John, the story of the good shepherd. After commenting on how attractive the shepherd-sheep analogy is to us politically and religiously, the leader of the worship says:

Those identified as sheep say to their political-religious shepherds: Your job is to take care of me. To feed me, shelter me, keep the baddies away, scratch my back, hold my sore paws, and pull out the uncomfortable burrs. In return for all of this I will allow you regularly to *fleece* me.

What if the shepherd-sheep analogy is a destructive one both for those who pretend to be shepherds and for those who pretend to be sheep? What if John, by placing Jesus in the role of the good shepherd, effectively explodes the meanings which that analogy previously carried. What if when John has Jesus say: "I am the good shepherd," the jig is up. The "I" gives its meaning to what follows rather than the reverse. Usually we begin with an idea of what the words "good shepherd" mean and apply the meaning backward to Jesus. It seems to me that by this method we may be making safe what would otherwise be revolutionary meanings in the New Testament.

Rather than the irresponsibility fostered by the shepherd-sheep analogy, the man from Nazareth calls all of us into the highest possible responsibility. He suggests that man living out of the trust that life is ultimately *for* man and seducing others to live their own, unique, responsible lives out of the same incredible trust, experiences the only security we shall ever know.

Pursuing *your* vision, living *your* life, you will discover why the man called Jesus paradoxically loved living so much that he was willing to be put to death rather than betray his life.

A prayer, a hymn, a benediction received with open eyes, since it is addressed to the people and not to God, and the first part of the service is over. There are no "greeters" at the doors. Those people you notice who call forth a response in you are yours to greet.

The second part of the morning, the forty-five-minute time for discussion, begins about fifteen minutes later with coffee in the library. After things settle down, the discussion begins with each person having an opportunity to introduce himself and make any initial comments he wishes. People respond very differently.

Seats are filled on all four walls with the string quartet, a secretary for the housing authority, a shift worker for a Texaco oil refinery, elementary schoolteachers, the personnel manager for a Philadelphia television station, several homemakers, several college professors, a personnel manager from Dupont, an engineer, the chairman of the West Jersey Presbytery's Commission on Religion and Race, a plant manager with his wife and teen-age daughter, the manager of the "Gold Bug"—a church sponsored coffeehouse—two folk singers from the Gold Bug, a number of college students and teen-age young people, a lighting equipment salesman, an eighty-five-year-old, longtime church member.

The father of the quartet, reflecting on the reference in the sermon to "living *your* life" mentions that two or three years ago he had become freshly aware of the fact that he would not live forever. He says he did not want to come to the end of his life wishing he had done something which was in his power to do. He tells of the decision to buy the farm and begin the music camp. At no point does he intimate that such a return to natural settings is the only way one can save his humanity in our increasingly urbanized and technological society. The plant manager speaks with equal feelings of his concern for the humanization of the industrial setting. As the discussion continues, it is evident that this concern for keeping life human matters deeply to most of the people in the room.

The theme and counterpoint type of discussion leads the observer to see that something unusual is happening casually and unself-consciously. People are speaking openly, on equal grounds, across lines drawn very clearly in our social structure. The union worker has a chance to say some things to the manager which he might never say in the typical, working context and vice versa. And so it is with college students and professors, staff members and heads of departments, teen-agers and parents, husbands and wives, men and women, Negroes and whites, young persons and the elderly.

Sometimes the discussion becomes very heated and angry;

at other times it is uncontrollably funny. It is never predictable, never manageable. The group is never made up of exactly the same people. At times the ideas of the sermon are vigorously attacked, other times largely ignored.

At 12:30 p.m., it is over, and people leave, most of them still talking in smaller groups.

What lies behind the experiences described? Like many groups in the past ten years this group began by concentrating on the question of what the church is and what it should be doing today. This search was strengthened by the cry from many sources that the church today was growing increasingly irrelevant, confused, and institutionally self-centered. Stripping down—leaving behind what appeared to be excess baggage—was the expression of the desire to discover what is essential.

Soon, it became apparent that even more basic questions needed to be faced. Not only did the group need to discover essentials concerning the nature and mission of the church, but it needed also to discover what was essential to all of us in terms of faith. What did we really believe, apart from what we had been told to believe, concerning God, Christ, the gospel, and so forth? More clarity at these points, we believed, would provide all of us with clues to what the contemporary church may be and may be doing.

It was on this road that the group came to what for us was a liberating insight. We discovered that, while our faith in Christ was real for us, the symbols that we used to attempt to communicate our faith were couched in supernatural thought forms which increasingly held no meaning for people living today, including ourselves. At this point, just because our faith meant so much, we wondered whether the abandonment of the supernatural framework might not result in the loss of the faith which was previously expressed *only* in such terms. Who ever knows exactly what it is which enables one to take such risks? Somehow we were enabled to make the leap. What followed has been increasingly a joy-filled surprise.

We learned what must have been clear to others long before us: The living experience of faith is not now and never was identical with the word and thought symbols used to express it. The effect was to make us even more eager to read the Scriptures for the root experiences which they reflect. It seemed clear that since the first Christians never wanted their inexpressible experiences with Jesus to become subsumed under or imprisoned in their choice of symbols, so any new means of communication we discover today will be subject to the same risk of misunderstanding in the future. The living Christ is always calling for new wineskins which contain but do not stop the fermentation. Each wineskin has its limit of stretching; the ever-new wine does not.

We found ourselves more able to give expression to what really mattered to us in the terms of our times. We found persons who had previously stumbled prematurely over our archaic thought forms, coming to the place where they could with integrity believe or reject the real stumbling block with which the Christian faith has always confronted men. Finally, we were more able to see the relationship between what matters most and the world in which we live, including our occupations, leisure time, and active commitments to civil rights, urban renewal, the war on poverty, the county hospital needs, and so on.

A member recently described this in a letter to a friend:

The sermons have dealt with the book of John. That version of the gospel I've pretty much left alone and wished that people around me would, too. But this fall I've heard John . . . as "episodes" or "symbols" in the life of a Man whose life took on increased meaning for mine. The interpretation was for the world I live in. I kept looking forward to the next installment and wondering where it would lead the discussion afterwards. A set of ideas was turning into a Person I wanted—not just ought—to follow.

Rather than dismissing as the aberrations of a prescientific society stories such as the raising of Lazarus, we ask ourselves what must have been the experience of the early Christians with Jesus which they could only express in such incredible terms? If there is nothing comparable in our lives, it may become expressive of our deepest longing and most hopeful expectation.

All this has enabled us to sit "loose" regarding many of the institutional structures which the modern church has inherited. Many of the practices and most of the architecture no longer communicate what we believe concerning Christ. In some cases, this will mean restoration of old forms; in others, it will call forth altogether new forms. We are just beginning to see the implications of what is happening for our children. This is a story in itself.

The mandate for this little congregation remains the same as it has always been for any Christian group: to follow the living Christ in our time according to the limits of our understanding of what this means. It is this inexpressible relationship which will give its own shape to our corporate life. Where it will take us we cannot imagine. The governing body of the church approved the following resolution on May 23, 1965, which says more what we no longer feel compelled to continue than what we now feel led to do:

We believe that God is leading our church into new paths, and we are willing as a Session to be led, though this may mean changing old and comfortable ways. This means that we are no longer necessarily committed to the maintenance, improvement, or restructuring of traditional forms of thought and practice in the church.

Much of what it all adds up to for us at the present time is found in these words of one of our members:

From the first, I would have said that this was the kind of church I wanted to be part of. At the beginning it was surprisingly easy to feel a part of the group, but there came a time when I started to recognize the costs. . . . Presbyterian in this town means something that's not entirely good to some of the people I listen to; identifying with this group has some hazards for a newcomer . . . . This church is so full of surprises—alive—serious and joyful. [The people] make no effort to hide their problems and weaknesses as a church, but offer so much that's worth taking chances for.

9

*See Ya Sunday!**

Mary F. Crawford

More and more retardates are being released from state schools
or institutions to return to their homes or communities to work.
Can we say that more churches are assuming their responsibilities by adding special church school classes, day camps, vacation
church schools, and youth fellowships for the retarded? Some
local churches are attempting to meet the challenge with weekday or Saturday classes in religious education, but this does
not always satisfy the retarded person. He has feelings about
Sunday as a day on which he sees his neighbors or other
members of his family go to church. "Why can't I attend church
on Sunday, too?" is a question he ponders.

Most educable retardates can be integrated in church programs, but this is not true of the "trainable" persons. These
need a segregated program, as usually they are socially as
well as mentally immature. In this article I shall refer to the
trainables whose I.Q.'s range from twenty-five to fifty and
who do not profit from the usual formal education. They can
be trained. however, in self-care, social adjustment, and economic usefulness. Some can become self-supporting.

Statistically, of every thousand persons, thirty are retarded.
Of that thirty, twenty-five are classified as educable, four as

* Originally published in the *International Journal of Religious Education*,
September, 1965.

trainable, and one as needing custodial care. Thus, the Greater Des Moines area (population over 250,000) would have approximately one thousand trainables among the mentally retarded. About sixty-five percent of these are in state schools or institutions. The remainder may be placed as follows:

> Public schools (city)............100
> Private Schools.................50
> Public schools (county).........30
> Foster homes, working in the city..100
> Living at home, preschoolers......100
>
> Total..380

There are three Sunday school classes for the retarded in Des Moines, two of which have been organized for several years. The third, organized as of spring, 1964, had five intermediate-age children. In 1964 Des Moines had two special vacation church schools, one sponsored by the local council of churches for children aged nine to thirteen, the other a class for teenagers.

For several years the Des Moines Council of Churches has had a committee for the retarded, guided by its director of Christian education. The committee of eight members includes parents, teachers, and ministers who are concerned about the religious needs of the mentally handicapped. Members have written for churches a brochure about the mentally retarded. They also conducted one of the vacation church schools mentioned above, besides volunteering their time to speak before different groups and helping to organize special classes on Sunday in local churches.

Last year this committee felt that the Greater Des Moines area needed a religious program that would reach more teen-agers and young adults sixteen and over, and help them know that the church doors are open to them, too. This program, it was agreed, should be held in a church on Sunday. From this initial planning the youth fellowship for the retarded developed the full-scale program it carries on today.

The major problem confronting the committee was to find curriculum materials that would be (1) acceptable to all denominations, and (2) on an elementary level of understanding without being too "kindergartenish." Most of the denominations were still in the progress of writing special materials which, therefore, were not available to us. However, we found some denominational weekday materials for the primary grades, parts of which we found usable for our group.

Much of the success of any program depends on a sufficient number of teachers. This is very true of a program for the retarded. It is recommended for young children that there should be one adult for three, and for older retardates there should be one adult for every eight.

Securing leaders, fortunately, was not a problem in our case. Three of the committee members taught in schools for the retarded, two others were the musically talented parents of a retarded girl, and the recreational leaders were college students with physical education majors or interested in special education. We also had three high-school students, one boy and two girls, who assisted the college students.

The parents of the high schoolers were most grateful for this experience for their sons and daughters. They said working with the retarded influenced their choice of college and majors. One is now in a YMCA college, one is majoring in special education, and the other is in nursing school. This meant that finding potential candidates for the youth fellowship was chiefly a matter of reaching parents. Not knowing what the response could be, we sent notes home with the children who were in school. The first Sunday nine showed up. The next

Sunday the number doubled. Currently, our enrollment is about twenty-five.

Because the hours were from four to six in the afternoon, it was easy to find a church that could accommodate us. The two-hour program made it worthwhile for parents to drive thirty miles round trip to transport a child—and many of them did.

The enthusiasm of the young people was spontaneous and immediate. Not a Monday morning went by after the first Sunday that Linda, aged twenty-four, did not stop at my classroom door in public school and yell, "Good morning, Miss Crawford. See ya Sunday!" as she went upstairs to her special class. Next, Bob, age twenty-six, would appear in my doorway, saying, "I hope I can go this Sunday night." Then John, peeking in and shaking his finger because he did not see me, would say: "Where are you hiding, Miss Crawford?"

A FOUR-PART PROGRAM

Our program was divided into four main parts: "singspiration," story and film, recreation, and lunch, with the last ten minutes reserved for closing thoughts.

For the "singspiration" we found song booklets that contained easy choruses and suitable songs. We avoided using nursery and kindergarten songs. A music supervisor said that nothing would mark a retarded child quicker than to hear him sing a kindergarten song, such as "Gray squirrel, gray squirrel, shake your bushy tail."

The music period was a happy one for the young people. It helped them to relax and enter into the spirit of Christian fellowship. I shall never forget Tom, a tall, lanky fellow of seventeen, who had returned home for the summer from a state school for the retarded. When visiting with Tom at various times, I found him noncommunicative and uninterested in my conversation. His mother told me she had observed the same behavior at home. What a joy it was to see him at our youth fellowship, participating wholeheartedly in the song service, his face beaming as he sang in a loud, lusty voice. He had found a way to release some of his emotions.

Seventeen-year-old Vera, short and chubby, sits in a trance when she hears music of any kind. Occasionally, she is able to sing a few words of a song. Her voice is lovely, very deep, and unusual for a girl of that age. One evening for our special music session, Vera sang her favorite song, one she had learned at school: "Swing Low, Sweet Chariot." We often have special music, instrumental, organ, electric guitars, and accordions— they love them all!

The thirty-minute block of time for our "story session" contained a number of activities. First, there was roll call, which gave members a feeling of importance as they heard their names called, and responded. Whenever possible we tried to develop this feeling of personal worthiness in the trainables. They are individuals, children of God as are other children, and should have the right to develop to the best of their capabilities. How often does a retarded child or young person receive a telephone call or a visitor who comes especially to see him or an assignment to run simple errands alone or to help plan some of the family activities?

After roll call the offering was taken by two of the members, a prayer followed, and then good news or telling time.

Telling or sharing time is very important to the retarded, for often in his home with all the family activities he is easily overlooked, and no one has time to listen to him. It is difficult for most retarded persons to communicate well enough to engage in an interesting conversation. So, it takes skill on the part of the leader to interpret the words of the retardate so the others will not lose interest.

It is amazing how a nonverbal, retarded person can communicate. One nineteen-year-old boy at good news time stood before the group and lifted his head and howled like a dog. We said, "Oh, you have a new dog." He gleefully nodded his head, snapped his fingers, and said, "Ya." We learned from questioning and from gestures that it was a big dog someone had given him. The dog slept on the floor in his bedroom. But the dog was homesick, and his parents were going to return him to the former owner in one day if he didn't stop howling (he held up one finger to tell us that!). We verified the story by asking his mother.

We introduced the newcomers and made announcements. Then we discussed the flat pictures on the bulletin board that related to the purpose for the session. Reading Bible verses followed, with one person holding the Bible. Occasionally one of the young persons would read a short verse. Several brought their Bibles with them each Sunday, including one of our Jewish boys (aged twenty-four), who placed his on the worship table with our Christian Bible.

In the session on "Helping God Care for His Beautiful World," we divided into three groups, each with an adult leader. Members talked about ways they could help and acted out these ways: (1) putting out the fire and picking up garbage on a picnic or weiner roast; (2) obeying signs in the park, like "Keep Off" and "Do Not Pick the Flowers"; and (3) putting trash in a litterbag when riding in a car.

A VISUAL-TYPE EDUCATION

We were able to show some beautiful films to correlate with the sessions on "God's Beautiful World," "Friends," and "God's Gifts of Sound, Light," These activities were particularly significant for retarded persons. Trainables do not learn from the printed word but depend wholly on visual learning and direct contact with other persons. Much depends on the adult leaders, parents, and teachers to be good examples for the young people and to present good ways of teaching.

During the recreation period our three physically handicapped who were unable to climb the steps to the gym would remain in the fellowship hall and count the offering and attendance, then report to the reassembled group at the snack period. Also, they would count out napkins and help prepare the food, which usually consisted of a fruit drink with either cookies, cupcakes, or potato chips. One boy brought cupcakes that he had made at home. Once we made ice cream as a group. Much valuable learning comes from eating together. Volunteers were always ready to set the table, count out napkins, assist the nonambulatory to take their places, and clean up afterwards.

We were careful not to select games that were too complex or long-drawn-out. In warmer weather we played outside. Volleyball, kickball, dodgeball, snatch-the-sock, and musical chairs were all favorites of this group. The fact that there were twice as many boys as girls accounted for the variety of ball games. One evening during an active game a girl came running over to me. Out of breath, but with a twinkle in her eye, she said, "Miss Crawford, I'm twenty-seven, and I'm getting too old to play this game." Then she laughed and said, "Oh, it's good for me," and ran back to join in the game.

The sessions ended worshipfully with a hymn, a recap of some of the learning experiences, and a closing prayer. Several times a leader suggested things for the young people to pray about silently and invited anyone to pray audibly if he desired.

Mary, who had spent all of her life in an institution and was now employed in a home, gave a prayer, simple in words but beautiful in giving thanks for the many blessings received. One evening our Jewish girl (aged twenty-seven) asked to say a Hebrew prayer that she had learned at her synagogue.

Then the last thing we did before departing was to stand in a circle, holding hands, and sing, "Blest Be the Tie That Binds." This seemed to have great spiritual significance for the retarded.

At our last meeting in May we decided that with the help of some parents we would have a banquet. For most this was a first experience. Everyone came in his best clothing, tables were beautifully decorated. There was delicious food and special music with our favorite accordionist. Small gifts were presented by our retardates to our student volunteers. As one boy stood to present a gift, he looked down at me and said, "Now, what do I say?" No one is embarrassed, for—you see—all understand one another.

Only four of our group were students in the public schools. One boy was from a state school and is employed in the community; another came from the suburbs. The others all attended the school sponsored by the local association for the retarded.

Somehow, doors open when people know that God's work is being done. As churches learned of our work, the contributions began coming in. These contributions have enabled our committee to add crafts to the program once a month.

Never before in my ten years of sponsorship of youth groups have I experienced the feeling of unity and fellowship that these mentally retarded young people have developed. They radiate brotherly love. As one leader put it, "They are so trusting and naïve that it's almost a sin to intrude into their thoughts." Just hearing them say with pride, "Our Youth Fellowship," is a joy. Now they can belong to an organization as other young people do.

10

The Night Ministry

William R. Grace

Ours is an urban nation. From 1790 to 1960 the urban population of the United States grew from 5.1 percent to 63.1 percent.
Such a statistic, however, is not just an interesting figure for
a course in applied mathematics. Rather, it constitutes an
expression of a massive change in man's life. Urbanization
is now the context for a radically different way of life—a way
of life which demands urban values, norms, and standards; a
way of life which has abruptly changed man's habits and
patterns; a way of life which reaches into every segment of the
human organism.

Perhaps the least perceived change in this urban way of life
is urban man's night life. No longer is darkness the time for
cessation of activity and retiring to the hearth. For some dusk
begins with the gulp of a quick dinner in order to attend another
round of endless committee meetings. Others are just arousing
themselves from a daylong slumber in order to prepare for
work. Some find the night a time for relaxation amidst the
countless forms of evening programs and entertainment. Many
find darkness a time for despair, loneliness, and fear. Still
others use the night as a time to confront the television, re-
plenished with beer and pretzels. And still others use the night
as a time for immorality and escape. Whatever the reason or
excuse, urban man does not consider the night a time to
gather around the hearth.

The rapid development of urbanization has meant literally that man's life must now embrace twenty-four hours. All of us are dependent upon those who work while we sleep; and our society would function badly without the morning paper, the morning milk, the night letters, the travel service, the postal service, and all the rest. Life is no longer contained in the daylight hours.

All of this, however, is to help the reader recognize that the church today cannot expect to minister to urban man through only a sixteen-hour day. Generally speaking, clergymen are available for counsel and help during the day hours—by appointment; but at night the committee structure makes a pastoral ministry all but impossible. To the man working from midnight until eight in the morning, roaming teen-age groups, the sobbing housewife in a hospital at three in the morning, the lonely, the afraid, and the countless numbers who find sleep impossible and the frightening darkness incoherent—the church is unavailable.

With this in mind—the high hope that a ministry at night would embrace much more than we could think—six Protestant denominations in San Francisco came together to support a night ministry. San Francisco, perhaps, was the ideal city to initiate such a ministry. Famous not only for its hills and cable cars, San Francisco has an already established night life. Restaurants and nightclubs are open seven days a week; neighborhood bars are open from 6:00 A.M. until 2:00 A.M. and the community is absolutely beautiful with its bright lights shining in the concrete valleys. After initial conversation and a trial period of thirty-two consecutive nights in the streets, bars, hospitals, and bus terminals, these six denominations became committed to the idea of a ministry at night.

In September of 1964 the Reverend Donald Stuart, of the United Church of Christ, was called to this most crucial, yet still experimental, ministry. His job description is very

simple, yet profound: to minister to men and women from 10:00
P.M. until 6:00 A.M. He walks a prescribed beat, in and out of
bars, all night beaneries, the police station, along skid row and
the tenderloin, among the gas station attendants and with the
countless numbers who just want to talk. In this context a
clergyman is available for any who need his services and skills
during the nighttime hours. The ministry is supported by over
sixty volunteers who, in teams of two, man the telephone to
answer calls from those in need or who want a minister at night.
The telephone number of the night ministry is in hotels, with
the cabbies, in bars, with the police, and so forth. The volunteers are trained to be skillful in handling the telephone and
relating the necessary information to the night minister when
he "calls in." This system of communication means that the
night minister is available to anyone in the city of San Francisco
within almost thirty minutes' time. And yet it does not force
the ministry of Don Stuart to sit and wait until the telephone
rings.

At this juncture it is necessary to point out clearly that this
is a ministry to people—all kinds of people—at night. It is
not a specialized ministry for just those dramatic incidents
such as suicide, alcoholism, drug addiction, prostitution, and
such. Although the ministry does involve itself in these human
needs, it is not directed solely to them. The night ministry is
a ministry to urban man and urban woman at night. It is
not just for the "outsider" but is also for those in need of
everything that is implied in the term "ministry."

Many of us with children, for example, are fully aware that
our children never seem to get sick at noon when energies
are not drained and nerves not sapped; but our children always
seem to get seriously ill at midnight when energies are sapped
and nerves are frayed. Think for a moment of answers to
this series of questions. Who ministers to the hotel and motel
clerks, who each and every night must make ethical judgments

regarding the truthfulness of couples seeking a room? Who ministers to the bartender? Who ministers to the paper boys standing on the corner? Who ministers to the travelers stranded in a strange city at night? These are not simply rhetorical questions. Each question is the actual context for the night ministry.

In this light, here is an actual incident that occurred during the night while I did "my tour of duty" as part of my commitment to this ministry. It was about three o'clock in the morning, and I was in the Mission Emergency Hospital in San Francisco's famed Mission District. A young woman was lying on a stretcher. Apparently she had either sprained her ankle severely or had broken it. Her husband was there, having brought her to the hospital. When I first observed this couple, the husband was standing over his wife and was attempting to calm her. He held her hand, stroked her forehead, and mumbled comforting words such as "The doctor will be here in a minute; don't worry; everything will be all right." Then he would go and sit down on one of the benches provided in the waiting room, smoke a cigarette, and then approach his wife with something like this, "I told you not to get up on that chair and fix the drapes . . . now look at the mess we are in."

This was perfectly human, normal, everyday experience, which is part of your life and mine; the only difference is that it occurred at night—a time when a ministry is normally not available; a time when few friends are around; a time which is very crucial in a marital couple's relationship; a time when the counsel of a clergyman is most desperately needed.

Now to be sure, the night ministry is a program that is structured for crisis. The person intent on suicide can be reached quickly, understanding can be brought to the lonely, a family with an alcoholic father can be helped as indicated. Nevertheless, in essence the night ministry is a pastoral ministry to people at night. Perhaps that which makes it acute is our fascination and fear when the sun goes down; perhaps it is a ministry on a new frontier simply because the church is seriously facing urbanization.

Whatever the reason, the night ministry is a biblically oriented ministry because the night belongs to God and constitutes still another battleground with the powers and principalities. God created the night. He ordained that there should be night as well as day. He led his chosen people through the wilderness by night. Jesus did miracles at night, prayed all night, and was betrayed at night. And remember Nicodemus? Nicodemus could only come to our Lord under the cover of darkness. The daytime was simply not the time to meet with the Christ. Is it too much to suggest that even in our modern, complex, technical society of today, there are many who can come to an awareness of themselves and the Christ of God only under the cover of darkness? [1]

[1] For more information regarding this significant ministry, the interested reader can write to: The San Francisco Council of Churches, 465 Post Street, San Francisco, California.

11

Giving Form to Feeling: Art and Communication

S. Thomas Leamon

Let us start with three truisms:

1. Persons frequently find it difficult, through lack of practice, to put their most meaningful thoughts and feelings into words.

2. A "built-in censor" inhibits us from putting our innermost selves—undefended and unarmored—at the mercy of others' judgments.

3. The church frequently aggravates the above two situations by encouraging the expression of "should" and "ought" attitudes, and by inhibiting the expression of how persons actually do think and feel. As a consequence:

a) Christian education frequently addresses itself to questions no one is asking, or irrelevant answers are given to unimportant questions.

b) Persons become convinced, despite the church's protestations to the contrary, that "the church is not interested in me as I really am. I cannot be myself in the church. I am neither good enough nor interesting enough to be a Christian, or (perhaps) to *be*."

The following pages describe five experiences in which the barriers to the communication of genuine feeling were significantly overcome. In each case the key to communication was found in the nonspecialized use of different art materials: clay, paint, collage.

COUNSELING WITH CHILDREN

A young mother, entering into unpleasant but well-justified divorce proceedings, becomes anxious about her daughter's basic attitudes toward the event. Does the little girl hate her father? Does she resent his leaving them? The daughter is an introspective seven-year-old of few words, and the mother cannot induce the child to share her real feelings. The mother brings the child to the pastor.

The pastor recalls the dramatic confrontation of the artist and the nonverbal bride described in Reuel Howe's book, *The Creative Years*, and he determines to use a lump of clay to enable the child to give form to her feelings. After some opening conversation the pastor invites the child "to show in the clay what your father is like." He said, "You don't have to make it look like him; just show how you feel about him. Do it any way you want to." With increasing absorption the child models a proud horseman under an arched canopy of clay. Considerable conversation ensues in which the threat of revealing deep personal feeling is largely diminished by the convenient reference to the clay "third-party object," and a significant spectrum of the child's real feelings is expressed, recognized, and dealt with.

It should be noted that the clay symbol by itself is seldom adequate as a full expression of feeling. It must be considered in the light of the child's words, physical attitudes, even silences. Since the interviewer must be initiated into the child's individual logic and symbolism, no question can be too simple or naïve: "Why is he on a horse?" "Why is he under the arch?" "Does he like being under there?" "What is the arch supposed to be?" "Does he feel lonely under there?" In this particular instance, the mother's fears proved unfounded. The child's real feelings communicated through the clay object showed her attitudes toward her father were robust and affectionate, despite the impending divorce.

CONFIRMATION TRAINING

Preparing to teach his eighth-grade confirmation class a unit on the Christian belief in God, the pastor prudently asked his group to interpret, in clay, their present concept of God. The class was a rather repressed and inexpressive group of small-town, rural youth, and nothing in the pastor's previous experience with the group had prepared him for the religious sophistication demonstrated in this project. One boy created an object, evidently surrealistic in the extreme: A human head, with beard and crew cut, loomed in front of a crude sun and a series of ocean waves.

The following is an excerpt of a tape made while the boy explained his symbol of God:

Boy: Well, see, this part here is the wild sea. And he's really ferocious. And he's got one Chinese eye and a moustache—which means that he can live in anybody. And over here—he's very happy: it's a daisy, sort of, in front of the sun—and he's smiling. And he's got an American eye, and he's got a real swingin' haircut like the Beatniks have, and he's got a goatee like my grandfather's.

Pastor: When you think of God, do you think of your grandfather—or do you think there is something of God in your grandfather?

111

Boy: Yes. He looks like him—what I think he looks like.

Pastor: So you think there's something in men that tells us something about God, and that God has different moods—he can be very happy or very ferocious or angry. . . .

Boy: And he can be very understanding. This Beatnik haircut means he can be very understanding even to them, and that he doesn't live in just the old world.

Pastor: What do you mean?

Boy: Well, some people think God only lived way back then, and that now he doesn't do anything. I don't know . . . I was kind of thinking of something else, but I'd have to have paints to do it.

Pastor: What would you do if you had paints?

Boy: Kind of make God like *love,* or something like that. It's hard to show in a symbol.

Member of class: God can be like water. Because water is all over the earth and he's all over the earth.

The vivid discussion, to which all members of the group felt deeply committed, moved on eventually into a comparison of a number of biblical symbols of God (Ezekiel's wheel, Moses' burning bush, the city of God of the Revelation) in which the class gave evidence of sharing a feeling of contemporaneity with the biblical symbol-makers.

DISCUSSION OF DOCTRINE WITH ADULTS

At a summer conference a group of laity and clergy was discussing the church. The leader of the group, wearied by the theoretical, uncommitted level of the discussion, brought the group down to earth by presenting them with a large can of clay. Following the lead of Chicago's Dr. Ross Snyder, he instructed the group, "Show how you feel about being a worker in the church." From this point on, vague generalities disappeared.

One woman showed a cluster of isolated bumps surmounted by tea cups, surrounded by a thick wall—the "lonely crowd" of her congregation, focused on social activities, walled-off from the life of the community at large. A young lawyer modeled a poignant upturned face, with no eyes, ears, or mouth. On the cheeks rested two, hard, small pellets. "I desperately need spiritual nourishment, but I'm not getting it in our church," he said. "My ability to express myself meaningfully has been frozen right out of me—even my despairing tears are solid ice!" His wife molded a recognizable beehive, with a tiny back porch containing a few bees. "Our church is a big beehive of well-organized activity. We love the church, but it gives us nothing real," she claimed. "I'm in a real dilemma—whether or not to get mindlessly involved in the hive, or to start sort of an annex with close friends who mean something to each other." One of the clergymen in the group made an assembly of freestanding figures, each very different in height and character; each standing on his own feet independently, with foundation underneath and an overarching "roof" which sheltered the community yet allowed unrestricted access in and out. The interpretation was hardly different from the description—a mature symbolization of the New Testament image of the church, in which the members are members one of another, bearing one another's burdens—each bearing his own burden. As the group members interpreted their clay symbols and expressed their real feelings about the church, the discussion passed naturally and meaningfully to the biblical images of the church and ways in which the biblical vision differed from the actualities expressed in clay, and, hopefully, promised a redeeming correction of them.

INSIGHT INTO THE PASTOR'S ROLE

A similar experience was shared by a clergy group. The materials and assignment were identical to those of the lay group described above, but where the laymen entered into the experience eagerly, the clergy were extremely reluctant and defensive when asked to express in clay their feelings about being workers in the church. Nevertheless, the men quickly became engrossed in the project, and a significant sharing of feeling and insights followed.

It became evident that several of the pastors had no clear identification of themselves as persons apart from their role as clergymen; their personal identity was equated with the identity of the church. On the other hand, one veteran clergyman symbolized himself as being outside the closed universe of his parish: "I don't know where I fit in here," he said. A campus chaplain produced a figure whose mouth, eyes, ears, cranium, and chest cavities were shockingly empty. On an arrow aiming into the figure were arranged seven ovoids, obviously intended for the empty spaces. "I have nothing good in myself," he explained. "Everything good in me—my hearing, seeing, saying, my brain, and guts—are all gifts from God. Without God I would be nothing." A spirited discussion followed on the topics of blurred identity, basic self-disparagement, and points at which pastors "fit in" to their parishes. The catharsis and deep level of communication among the men produced a rare atmosphere of koinonia and fellow-feeling out of an experience that the men had initially dreaded.

DEVELOPMENTAL TASKS OF ADOLESCENTS

A related, but a more specialized, experience in communication is the making of *self-portraits* with adolescents. The collage technique is used instead of clay. Commonplace materials and cut-and-paste methods of assemblage are deliberately used to encourage confidence among those who cannot think of themselves as artists. Those participating should bring an armload of old magazines of any and all kinds, scissors, paste, a muffin tin (to serve as a multiple-unit watercolor palette), a couple of old cellulose sponges which, cut up, serve as "brushes" for applying paint, and an old can for water. The host institution (church, youth group, summer conference, retreat) can supply large (22" x 28") sheets of poster board and jars of dry pigment or poster paint in a number of basic hues. Supplementary materials may be used, suggestive of various moods or feelings (tacks, cotton batting, ribbon, wire, lace, sandpaper, sand, or dirt, and so forth).

There are several essential conditions to presenting the project.

First, the group should be led to think together about the multidimensional complexity of any one human life—its diffuse roots, its uniquely varied past, the combination of hopes and fears, opportunities, and predetermined patterns that make up the future, the options and situations of the present. It can well be pointed out how very different one's life appears to one's self, parents, friends, enemies, teachers, and so on. Then the problem should be posed: "We want you to depict your life, now, as you feel it to be, as you alone know it to be."

Second, it is imperative that no sample self-portraits be shown the group beforehand. To do so curtails the freedom of creation which is one of the prime benefits of this activity. Say to the group, "There is no *right* way to do it. Do it any way you wish, with any of these materials or anything else you can think of." (One high-school student has exclaimed, "We can make a mess and no one will say anything! We've never done this before!") It is advisable to suggest to the group basic techniques, such as clipping pictures or parts of

115

pictures from magazines and combining them with words or parts of words cut from type. Tacks, dirt, ribbon may be glued to the surface in combination with paint. Holes may be cut in the board, or constructions made on it.

Third, insist on silence during the period allotted for working. Separate the participants as much as possible to insure originality. But never insist that young people "get busy and get to work." One of the most explosive, pregnant self-portraits was done by a junior-high boy who gazed fixedly at his empty cardboard for two mornings, until, half an hour before the time was up, he erupted into action with a felt-pen marker, creating a self-portrait loaded with symbols of intense anxiety, tension, hostility, and sexual confusion.

Fourth, insist that as many adult advisors as possible participate fully in the project, despite any objections. A summer conference counselor almost had to be forced to do a self-portrait, but she became so absorbed in the process that at the end, after the leader's third request to rejoin the group went unheeded, she had to be literally lifted from her work. As the leader approached, the counselor was heard to mutter wonderingly to herself, "My husband just wouldn't recognize me at all from this!" The value of adult participation is that it enables teens to see that adults share with them the same humanity; that they—the adolescents—are not freaks but members of the human race after all. A clergyman was able to point to the great clenched fist he had pasted in the center of his self-portrait and say to the teen with whom he was talking, "You see, I, too, have a lot of anger at the center of my life, just as you have; and, like you, I have to learn acceptable ways of handling and understanding it." This sharing of inner worlds is of the essence of the nature of the church, and it has proved to be a genuinely redemptive encounter in the relationship just described.

The self-portrait experience can be concluded in one of

two ways. With small groups the entire group of portraits can be spread out for discussion and mutual explanation. In large groups one adult and a few teens can gather in small discussion groups or cells to interpret self-portraits to one another; then, possibly the entire group can share any general insights or conclusions reached by the various subgroups. In no case should interpretation be forced or compulsory. If anyone prefers not to comment on his creation, this preference should be respected. In both cases it is effective and significant, in concluding, for the leader to make the following summation: There is not one self-portrait here that is not interesting—each one is colorful and of great interest; it is extremely difficult to say that one is "better" or "worse" than another. God sees us as individuals of varying patterns, each interesting and colorful. Each one has a right to coexist in the company of the others. All, young and old, share the hopes and fears, the victories and defeats, illustrated by the self-portraits. Thus, in a real sense, this is an illustration of the church. God does not evaluate us as "black or white," good or bad.

A few illustrations and observations follow, now, which indicate some of the uses, benefits, and opportunities of this procedure. The project can be used to study specific Christian doctrine. A parochial school student, making self-portraits with a Protestant Sunday evening youth group, observed, "There isn't anything in these portraits to show that the persons are Christian or even religious." Another member of the group responded, "God is in the background of all the things." An important discussion followed on what a genuinely Christian self-portrait would look like and at what point Christian faith touched the items represented in the self-portraits (a flashy sports car, a bottle of Scotch, a glamorous bride). At the weekend retreat a high-school girl made a series of concentric, color-coded rings around a cross—which represented God in the center of life. Nearest to God was a green ring, representing

117

the world of nature and natural beauty; next was a ring of orange, representing friendships and parties. The third ring was red and quite agitated; it stood for the hurly-burly and pressure of school life. On the circumference, farthest from "God" was a ring of black. It symbolized the wars, violence, threats of the world. Although this diagram was an evasion of the self-portrait assignment, it did spark a highly valuable discussion about God's presence in the world, as well as a study of Amos, Isaiah, and Jeremiah—and Jesus—and the students, perceptions as to where and how God is at work.

It can be seen from the foregoing how self-portraits can be used to make up a series of programs for a youth group. The material expressed, the concerns revealed in the portraits become the material around which the youth programs are constructed for the following year. During the period the self-portraits could remain on the wall of the meetingplace to remind the group of the life context of their programs.

Self-portraits can serve as catalysts for redemptive insight. An attractive, intelligent, and talented high-school junior depicted herself as a tiny, isolated silhouette chained in the middle of her world. Her feet were enormous. Haltingly, she put into words her dissatisfaction with herself, her feelings of insufficiency and of being disliked—and her feeling of ugliness because of large feet! The spontaneous expression of astonishment on the part of the group went a long way toward reassuring the girl that she was in fact admired and respected and, not least, that her imagined ugliness was indeed imagined. It is inconceivable that such matters, with their festering importance to the girl herself, would have ever been brought into the light without the symbolic presence of the self-portraits.

A pastor received vital insight through a self-portrait. An awkward, poorly adjusted high-school boy, conspicuous because of size and odd behavior, created a fearful complex of rifles, swastikas, blots, smears, and staring eyes in red and black.

The fury of the symbols alerted the pastor that the boy's disturbance went much deeper than superficial rebellion. Through the conversations revolving around the self-portrait the pastor was able to create and sustain an atmosphere of confidence that played an important role in supporting the boy and his family through subsequent robbery, attempted suicide, self-commitment to a mental hospital, and a heroic effort to find eventual employment. While it must be said forcefully that self-portraits are in no sense a "layman's Rorschach test," in no way an adequate psychological or psychiatric testing device, they can serve as a medium which, taken in the context of the manner and content of the creator's interpretation, makes possible a deeper and more meaningful level of personal communication and understanding than is possible by words alone. Possibly the most valid function of the self-portrait process is in helping youth achieve an answer to the question "Who Am I?"—which the psychiatrist Erik H. Erikson indicates is the central developmental issue for adolescents. The following words from an essay written by a former youth fellowship member for a university freshman English class verify, without need of comment, the claim made above:

My self-analysis did not begin with the preparation for writing this essay. On the contrary, it began several years before, when I was a member of a youth group. The programs which I became involved in as a member of this group enabled me to step back and take a long, searching look at what I actually am, what I think about certain issues, and what I believe both spiritually (in the sense of religion) and prospectively as concerns my role in life. One of the programs which interested me most was the creation of self-portraits. . . . I was able to learn an amazing amount about myself through an honest self-portrait. After this initial discovery of my true self, the discoveries to follow were much easier. I found myself evaluating my reactions during times of crisis . . . and becoming aware that I have not only faults, but strengths.

119

The young man proceeds to list his strengths and weaknesses, his limitations and advantages, and exhibits an admirable balance of self-awareness, justifiable pride and healthy humility, a thoroughly appropriate measure of independence and dependence, of personal potential and social responsibility. The young man himself exhibits many of the distinctive Christian virtues and values we cherish for those who have passed through our churches, and in his person he validates the crucial importance of the kind of communication we have been discussing in this chapter.

One presupposition lies behind each of the five modes of communication. It is this. The loving, accepting, and enlivening Spirit of God, promised by Jesus to his church, is not manifested essentially through "religious" assertions imposed from "outside" to which we fit the date of our lives where and if we can. On the contrary, God is at work in life-as-it-is, in the light and shadow of our daily dreads, hopes, regrets, celebrations, ideas, defeats, and accomplishments. In recognizing and sharing these movements and currents of our lives now—in giving them concrete form—we find the Spirit of God taking shape in our midst and building the community which is his primary work.

12

Biblical Concepts Through Contemporary Literature

Arthur L. Reed

THE PROBLEM

There is evidence that the church may now be at the dawn of an age of new and deeper understanding. Some may feel it more realistic to say that the church is not yet at this point. Nevertheless, it seems certain beyond a doubt that our age is one in which the biblical message is in general hidden and lost. To continue the metaphor, some may feel that the church has yet to see the dawn of light, and they question if it will or not. A critical factor is whether the people communicating the Christian message to others will put it in a form which may be understood and, more important, actually experienced by people living today.

Just as in earlier ages, our age is faced with the great problem of the biblical message being hidden or lost. For the most part, our biblical language is without meaning for people of the modern world. There is, of course, the handful of dedicated laymen which has managed to sift out the message in spite of all difficulty with archaic, meaningless language from another age and culture. Beyond them is the much larger group of active church people who, through less fault of their own perhaps than those presenting the message, has not really been able to experience the "good news" of the gospel. Beyond this group come the masses of our population which for the most part claim membership in a church when the polls are taken, but reject any real affiliation and find the church rather meaningless or downright nonsense in relation to their everyday life.

Active church people today have been taught to express their faith in traditional terms of the Bible and theology. For example, when we speak of Jesus Christ and his meaning for us, it is usually stated that he is our Savior, Lord, Master, or Teacher. It is often stated further that he has saved us from sin and brings us to eternal life. He has redeemed us and brought us from death to life or to the kingdom of God. The problem is that in most cases people are repeating intellectually a message which is not related to their life and experience. Proof of this fact lies in the failure of people to be able to take the biblical and theological symbols and translate them into modern, everyday language and experience.

For example, when Jesus is described as "Savior" or "Lord" it is important to say just what this means and to give an example of how he has functioned as Savior or Lord in modern-life situation. When one discusses "redemption" and the "kingdom," it is likewise important to describe these symbols in modern language and everyday experiences of our modern world. Very rarely is it possible for people today to translate the traditional language of faith into modern language and experience, and thus these statements have deteriorated into biblical and theological jargon without meaning.

THE GOAL

The use of modern novels, short stories, and drama will lead people to experience aspects of the Christian life now only spoken of intellectually in biblical and theological language. All biblical and theological words as mentioned above are

122

symbols of experience in everyday life. All these religious experiences are enacted in the art forms throughout the ages, and *modern* writings, among other art forms, come closest to the understanding and lives of the present generation.

Reading literature and drama which contain experiences identical to those being described in the Bible will bring a deep emotional involvement with the experience. The reader will identify very personally with the characters and relive experiences in his own life which are comparable. This rarely happens to laymen reading the Bible. The lack of understanding of biblical words on the experiential level keeps most readers from identification and deep involvement with the message. Erroneous definitions of biblical concepts which have developed through the centuries likewise obscure the real meaning. Those who are theologically trained may relate a greater amount of the biblical text on the experiential level. Nevertheless, it has been this writer's experience that the most meaningful messages of the Bible must still be "translated" into modern experiences or sequences for deepest emotional involvement.

The situation may be compared very appropriately to learning a foreign language. For a long duration of one's training in a language the student will automatically translate the foreign language into his native tongue in order to understand and experience the word or writing. It takes many years to think and actually live in the new language. It is indeed a difficult and long process. Our goal in Christian education is to begin by translating the message into the "native" experiences of the people of this century. A foreign language class would not keep students very long if it merely taught them to pronounce the foreign vocabulary and read the literature without translation and understanding. Yet, this is what the church does to a very great degree by failing to "translate" the biblical experiences into modern ones as found in contemporary literature and other art forms.

After experiences are identified in modern literature, related to one's life, and expressed in one's own vocabulary, the next step is to identify them with experiences from the biblical text. Then the theological concepts come alive. The biblical ideas about man, God, faith, sin, salvation, and Jesus as the Christ are transformed from the abstract word to a living experience for the reader. At this point the Christian message begins to relate to life and take on deep meaning. Only at this point is a person really grappling with himself and Christianity.

THE METHOD: CHRISTIAN FAITH EXPRESSED IN CONTEMPORARY LITERATURE

As the experiences of the characters of modern literature are reenacted in the mind and life experiences of the reader, he is deeply confronted by many aspects of Christianity. Faith is almost always defined by Christians as knowledge or a body of doctrine to be studied and learned. Faith so defined remains on the intellectual level, unrelated to one's life and quite contrary to faith as defined by modern theologians such as Paul Tillich and H. Richard Niebuhr who define faith, in the biblical text, as one's ultimate concern[1] or one's object of loyalty.[2] For example, the whole basis of Israel's religion was in covenants or promises between God and his people. For Jesus, the trust he had for his creator was the whole basis of his living.[3]

Examples from short stories and drama, suitable for a confirmation class, which lead students to a biblical concept of faith as ultimate concern or trust in God alone are many and varied.

In "Pigeon Feathers," a short story by John Updike, David,

[1] Paul Tillich, *Dynamics of Faith* (New York: Harper & Row, 1958), pp. 1 ff.

[2] H. Richard Niebuhr, *Radical Monotheism and Western Culture* (New York: Harper & Row, 1953), p. 16.

[3] *Ibid.*, pp. 41-42.

a confused teen-ager, is accompanied by the reader through the very disturbing experience of questioning and doubting his insecure faith based on knowledge and facts of the Bible.[4] as he seeks a new security and basis of faith from his mother, father, and minister, one after another, he finds them all to be inadequate due to their uncertainties. Even though he still ends up "robed in this certainty" (i.e. the certainty of eternal life), he moves a big step closer to trust in God. Trust in God finally must accept uncertainty. A ninth-grade student wrote the following about the story: "I don't believe that is the end of the story. David's last thought was his last grasp on his boyhood concepts. I think he was getting a finale on a dream that would wake him up and nudge him into sincere and deep personal concepts of God and heaven."[5]

Tennessee Williams' *Case of the Crushed Petunias* is another example of faith. It is especially good for and popular with teen-agers because the symbolism is quite obvious. Dorothy Simple lives with faith and trust in her notions business and has "barricaded her house and her heart behind a double row of petunias."[6] After much resistance and many excuses she musters the great amount of courage necessary to get outside her secure, but dead, little world and face a world of uncertainty and possible danger. If it is thought that such a faith has nothing to do with "Christian" faith or faith in God, it may be noted that the world is considered by Christians to be God's creation. Doubting and distrusting God's world cannot be separated from one's attitude and action toward God.

The Concept of Sin in Literature

The concept of man as sinner is very basic to the Bible but often overlooked and denied in all periods of history. Beginning

---

[4] John Updike, *Pigeon Feathers and Other Stories* (Fawcett, 1963), pp. 84 ff.

[5] Joan Carey, student manuscript.

[6] *Ten Short Plays*, ed. by Jerry M. Weiss (Dell, 1963), pp. 31 ff.

with the stories of Adam, Cain and Abel, Noah and Moses, right through the New Testament, the whole drama is about man's turning against God who, nevertheless, accepts him and forgives him in spite of his ways.

"Between Rounds" expresses the above concept of man's nature and includes the possible positive action for man as well.[7] Mr. and Mrs. McCaskey's life together is a constant fight. One round of the battle is interrupted when a neighbor child in the big city apartment where they live is lost. For a few minutes the childless couple become more tender toward one another and discuss what they would have named a child had they been blessed with one. Soon a remark is made by one, and the fight is in a new round again.

Wilder's *Skin of Our Teeth* is a play based on the biblical characters of Adam and Eve, Cain and Abel.[8] It conveys in dramatic fashion the nature of man as a sinner who also has the faith or courage to "pick up the pieces" and carry on in spite of what might have befallen him.

Judgment and Salvation in Literature

The biblical message of salvation is of imperative importance. Of what use is all one's preaching and teaching if the student does not understand how he is saved? John Updike deals beautifully with the problem of salvation in the short story, "Lifeguard." In this parable a divinity student spends the summer as a lifeguard on the beach. He states: "We struggle and thrash, and drown; we succumb, even in despair, and float and are saved. . . . Someday my alertness will bear fruit; from near the horizon there will arise, delicious, translucent, like a green bell above the water, the call for help, the call,

[7] O. Henry, *The Four Million and Other Stories* (Airmont, 1963), pp. 30 ff.

[8] Thornton Wilder, *Three Plays* (Bantam Books, 1958), pp. 65 ff.

a call, it saddens me to confess, that I have yet to hear." [9]

Thus, the acceptance of salvation depends on one's attitude rather than the more often described problem of intellectual understanding. There is much human resistance to succumbing, even in despair, and floating. We are all more inclined to desire continued struggle and thrashing. It is the universal problem of man that he grasps at any straw in the wind which may lead him away from the despair of admitting his own shortcomings and confessing his ways.

As long as one reads from the biblical text, the escape from conviction of sin is fairly easy. But alas, the loss of salvation is the more tragic because one has not even been able to choose for or against it. It is distressing that there is no call for help. As long as one continues to use the traditional words which have not related to everyday experience, the message will very easily be obscured by problems of intellectual understanding, cultural differences, and the defenses against accepting judgment.

With the use of modern literature the intellectual and cultural problems are overcome for the most part, leaving only the wall of defense to penetrate in order to bring one to decision for or against the acceptance of sin and salvation.

For example, Dorothy Simple, in *The Case of the Crushed Petunias*, has decided to accept the judgment on her "deadly" life in the notions shop and *do* something about it. The road to "Life Incorporated" is described in the following way:

It is in an awful condition, overgrown by brambles! . . . . The moon at night makes such confusing shadows people lose their way, go dangerous places, do outrageous things. . . . senseless acrobatics, cart-wheels in mid-air, unheard of songs they sing, distil the midnight vapors into wine—do pagan dances! [10]

[9] *Pigeon Feathers and Other Stories*, pp. 147 ff.
[10] *Ten Short Plays*, pp. 52-53.

Jesus and his followers have been described in similar fashion in the Bible as have Christians throughout the ages.

Another example of a salvation experience is in Thornton Wilder's *Our Town*. Emily dies, goes to the cemetery on the hill, and joins those who have passed on before. Her request to return to life for one day is granted with misgivings, and she chooses her twelfth birthday to relive. But she is entirely different from before. Those already dead now realize many things:

Live people don't understand, do they?

You not only live it [life]; but you watch yourself living it.

Do any human beings ever realize life while they live it?—every minute?

No . . . the saints and poets, maybe—they do some.

Now you know—that's the happy existence you wanted to go back to. Ignorance and blindness.[11]

Scriptural parallels to the salvation experience of Emily abound. In the fourth chapter of Mark, when the parable of the sower is told, Jesus was speaking to a worldly audience like the one in *Our Town*. Jesus said: "To you has been given the secret of the kingdom of God, but for those outside everything is in parables; so that they may indeed see but not perceive, and may indeed hear but not understand; lest they should turn again, and be forgiven." (Mark 4:11-12.)

The Gospel goes on to describe how hard the words of salvation are to listen to and to live. "The cares of the world, and the delight in riches, and the desire for other things, enter in and choke the word." (Mark 4:19.)

The characters of *Our Town* and *The Case of the Crushed Petunias* may be compared very easily to the "man who was

---

[11] *Three Plays*, pp. 56-63.

deaf and had an impediment in his speech" (Mark 7:32) and was cured by Jesus. It was no different from Emily's and Dorothy's being cured of their "deafness and blindness" to what was really important in life.

The Concepts of Death and Resurrection in Literature

The concepts of death and resurrection are likewise expressed in these stories. These are very common occurrences in literature. These characters may be seen as being resurrected from death to life. Tennessee Williams refers to "Death, Unlimited," and "Life, Incorporated." The change in Dorothy Simple is indeed a "dying" to her old way of life and starting a new "living way." Emily had died in order to gain a new perspective on life. The hope, of course, is that the reader will not wait until he is in the cemetery to live in a new spirit but will "die to his present way of living" in his subsequent decisions.

The Concept of Jesus as the Christ in Literature

The concept of "Jesus as the Christ" is also present in modern literature. Like the concept of salvation, this concept is very important in Christian education since the Christ is the *bearer* of salvation. The question of great importance asked by Jesus in the gospels is "Who do you say that I am?" Peter answered, "You are the Christ." [12] For the scribes and Pharisees, Jesus was not the Christ. For many who followed him listening but remaining blind and deaf to his message, he was not the Christ. For Pilate, he was not the Christ. Jesus could not function as the Christ for those who did not come to a new conviction about their lives and their decisions. If they did not really hear and apply his message to themselves, they could not receive salvation.[13] But for Peter, Jesus was the Christ.

[12] See Paul Tillich, *Systematic Theology*, II (Chicago: The University of Chicago Press, 1957), 97 ff.
[13] See Gerald H. Slusser, *The Local Church in Transition* (Philadelphia: The Westminster Press, 1964), pp. 147 ff.

In order for Jesus to function as the Christ for either his contemporaries or for someone of any period, he must bring to their personal lives a new judgment and enable them to come to a decision for a radically new life. One's present life must be seen as inadequate, meaningless, and deadly. An opportunity must be presented for a new way of living. This new life is referred to as the presence of the kingdom of God or heaven and in John's gospel as eternal life. Its coming is considered inevitable, just as the inevitable growth of a mustard seed.[14] Anyone who functions in another's life to bring about the radical conversion from a "dead" to a "living" existence would act as a savior for that person. Characters in literature who seek to bring another to this new life will not likely be very popular. They may be faced with crucifixion of one form or another. At least, they are greeted with no great love by many and probably much hostility instead.

The young man who walked on Dorothy Simple's protective row of flowers was not "worshipped as the son of God." He was treated more like Jesus when she called the police officer. He was referred to as a dangerous maniac at large who might also be "equally capable . . . of striking a helpless woman or kicking an innocent child!" [15] Nevertheless, it was the young man who brought the word of judgment to Dorothy Simple's life and enabled her to choose salvation or a new life. He revealed the "idolatrous" nature of her life and spoke of an alternative.

The Gospel According to Peanuts, although theology rather than literature, is among the best material available to students trying to understand the concepts of judgment, salvation, and the Christ as bearer of these. Robert L. Short's first chapter

[14] See Rudolf Bultmann, *Jesus and the Word* (New York: Charles Scribner's Sons, 1934), p. 38.
[15] *Ten Short Plays*, pp. 34-35.

deals with the use of modern art forms in conveying the Christian message. He aptly includes the cartoon along with the literature that has been discussed as a valid and meaningful mode of presentation of biblical concepts today. The message concerns the various characters of the cartoon, each of whom have their idols according to the author. Linus "worships" his blanket; Charlie Brown, his desire to win; Schroeder's god is Beethoven, and Lucy's god is Schroeder.[16] Snoopy, the dog, is the character which acts as "the Christ" in the situation. He not only reveals the others' idolatry to them; but he is humble, lowly, devoted, and joyful. He is a servant to all.

Thus, these are a few examples of contemporary literature which bring people to an experience of the gospel message. If we follow the message and its verbal expression in the modern, everyday language of experience, it becomes much easier to turn to contemporary theology and finally to the Bible itself for real understanding. Once the student has a few models of Christian experience from modern literature and is able to "translate" the biblical language and concepts himself, he has mastered the basic skill of understanding the Bible. It has been this writer's very rewarding experience to find this the case with two ninth-grade confirmation classes which followed this type of curriculum.

The Church and Community Reaction

Youth become greatly fascinated by developing the skill of understanding biblical terms and being able to relate them to their own experience. But there are other reactions in addition to fascination. During study of the first unit of the course when the short stories were being read, there was a rather prevalent need on the part of the students to categorize the

---

[16] Robert L. Short, *The Gospel According to Peanuts* (Richmond: John Knox Press, 1964), pp. 34 ff.

characters in the stories as "odd, disturbed, neurotic, and abnormal." This allowed them to place themselves safely in a category of "normalcy" and evade any feeling of judgment. The stronger the personal judgment and identification, the more emotional was the student reaction against the character being discussed. A good example was "David" in "Pigeon Feathers."

It was necessary at first for about half of the students to disagree strongly with stories bringing judgment to man or stories describing him as evil. This need was strongest among students who had begun the course with a philosophy of man's goodness already well developed. The Bible message had never been this devastating to their basis of faith since the message had been well disguised in less understandable language and presentation. But in contemporary literature the nature of man as sinner was devastating to the security of quite a few. Their basis of faith in the goodness of man was questioned.

Not until about the eighth month of the course did the resistance to man's goodness seem to crumble almost completely. By this time the message had been covered at least three times, in modern short stories, in contemporary theology, and in the Bible.

At the end of the course the students were asked to write an essay about their reaction to the confirmation experience. They were given the option of submitting them anonymously and were told that their comments would have no bearing on their passing the course or being eligible for church membership. Negative comments were solicited as well as positive for a more meaningful evaluation of the experimental course.

The comments which were stated most frequently are listed below in the order of the frequency of mention by the students. There were twenty-three students in two classes of nine and fourteen students. Each student wrote the essay.

Student Reactions to Confirmation

Positive Comments

Twelve liked most of the material most of the time.

Nine liked *The Gospel According to Peanuts* the best.

Ten liked the various short stories and plays.

Seven thought the course was different from any they had ever had. (Supplementary comments gave a positive note.)

Six liked the study about man and the world.

Four liked the one-hour weekly class discussions.

Three liked the unit applying the material to the Bible.

Three thought the course should be for two years rather than only one.

Three liked selections from Bultmann's *Jesus and the Word*.

Three liked the Bible selections.

Three liked the chapters from *My Confirmation*.

Two liked the course for not dealing so much with religion, God, and the Bible.

Negative Comments

Two thought the material was boring.

One did not like the short stories and plays.

Three did not like the study about man and the world.

One did not like the discussions.

One did not like the biblical application.

Three thought that one year was too long and that the previous course of six weeks was enough.

Three did not like *Jesus and the Word.*

One did not like the Bible selections.

Two did not like *My Confirmation.*

Six thought the course did not relate enough to religion, God, and the Bible.

Three thought the material should be easier to understand.

Three would have preferred not having the weekly homework of reading and writing.

In summary, *The Gospel According to Peanuts* was the most effective book of the course according to the students. The instructor is in agreement as well. Only the class of fourteen used this book which makes the total of nine comments a higher ratio than the following comment of ten out of twenty-four students who mentioned liking the short stories. We felt this was a fairly good response. Quite a few students felt the course significant enough to mention how different it was from any other educational experience.

Confusion seems to be evidenced by the response to the study of man and the world in contrast to the more traditional method of studying religion, God, and the Bible primarily. Six students mirrored the more traditional approach by feeling that the course did not relate enough to religion, God, and the Bible. Deeper understanding of biblical concepts was sought by utilizing the short stories and plays. Nevertheless, a few still felt that they were not studying religion.

All the confusion over relating man and the world to religion seems to support the present course structure. The goal spoken of previously is to lead people to experience aspects of the Christian life now only spoken of intellectually in biblical and theological language. In spite of the repetition of the basic biblical concepts in literature and drama, elementary theology, and finally the Bible itself, the bridging of life and religion remains very difficult for a few.

The experiences of all the short story and drama characters are real and interesting, but the stereotype of traditional religious education was not easy to overcome. If experiences do not relate to church, worship, or specific biblical vocabulary, they are often relegated to the secular or nonreligious. Nothing could be more damaging to Christian education. However, since only one-fourth of the students made this comment and most of them are able to relate religion and the short stories, progress is evident.

The final essays of the students dealing with the "contrast between true faith, bringing life and resurrection, to false faith, bringing death" were most rewarding to read. Several quotes from student manuscripts will show the ability to interpret the religious symbols in everyday language and to identify with the experiences in the short stories and plays.

Take, for example [concerning idol worship], a person who idolizes boats. He saves his money and gets a boat of his own. This is fine, he thinks, until the boat is old and rotten. He loses his god. This results in spiritual death.[17]

This [topical statement] is a very symbolic statement. This means that faith in God brings happiness and a clean conscience . . . . The biggest example of this is a play called *Our Town*. In this play a person dies and experiences resurrection in a symbolic sense. We experience resurrection in a symbolic sense, while we're alive. Another example of this is *The Case of the Crushed Petunias*. In this story a woman has false faith in her story and material things (her petunias). The resurrection comes when she is brought to destroy her material things in life and have faith in life. Here is a good comparison which shows her living in death till she has true faith when she lives again. In the "Story of the King" [Graham

[17] Sue Aiken, student manuscript.

Greene] a man has false faith and suffers his death in his conscience, and when he realizes his true faith and comes to it, he sees his wrong ways and lives again. In this example, life wins out again.[18]

When we talk of death in this sense, we don't mean physical death, but a living death (hell on earth), every day which comes from finding that the things or people we had our faith in have let us down or can't give us what we really need. We must learn to have faith in God first and then we can find the right place in our lives for the people or things that are important to us. We have to learn by our mistakes and often become very discouraged and unhappy before we can learn to have the right kind of faith (in God). This kind of faith is like "being born again" or resurrection.[19]

I don't believe that you should worship idols because they can be destroyed by wind, rain, and nature, because no idol can last forever like God can.[20]

False faith bringing death is when a person worships something that will not last and you can't trust in because it is not a steady object as God is.[21]

It is worth striving for life and putting aside idols. Death is centered around ourselves. In *The Case of the Crushed Petunias*, the woman lived in a world revolving around herself. It took something drastic to draw her out of her shell and bring her into the world of God. There can be no in-between, or state of indifference, because this indifference is sin and death . . . . *Our Town* points out the goodness of life and obedience to God. It shows how ignorant and unappreciative we really are in our attitude to fellow man and God.[22]

[18] Randi Decater, student manuscript.
[19] Andrew Foote, student manuscript.
[20] Joseph Lattin, student manuscript.
[21] William Leibold, student manuscript.
[22] Joan Linley, student manuscript.

True faith can be considered as complete and utter devotion to God and love of God and man. . . . This way you have life instead of existence. . . . This is resurrection. It occurs during life, not after death. Jesus lived a life of true faith. It was free of idols. He preached good news of the gospel and resurrection. One's trust and faith is beyond the idols of the world. He demonstrated this by facing the cross. Had he continued to live on earth, he wouldn't have lived later with the people of today. The crucifixion is the first symbol of Christianity gained by loss. It was the final test . . . . In the *Story of the King* he lived a life of self-centeredness, self-love, and idols. His money, women, and other idols were his whole life; of course, he was the main factor. He didn't care about anyone but himself and his beliefs. He never observed the happenings around him—only the changes in his bank account and other "absurd" and selfish thoughts. These all led him to a death.[23]

In the course the basic biblical concepts of man, God, sin, salvation, faith, and Jesus as the Christ are all touched upon at least, and in general expanded upon, in relation to everyday life and experience. There seems little question about man's inclination to idol worship or an acceptance of this as his shortcoming or sin. The possibility of salvation, also spoken of as life or resurrection, is likewise a possibility for man in his everyday life. This is in great contrast to the absurd theological concept of Jesus' substitutionary atonement—bringing salvation to man in some magical or supernatural manner through his life and having absolutely no relationship to the individual's life and decisions. This is in no way denying Jesus' divinity or saving power, but qualifies the manner in which the power must be actualized by each individual in his own life.

Some mention of the adult reaction to the course is noteworthy. Adult criticism of this approach to confirmation has centered to a great degree upon the concept of man. It is believed by some that emphasis should not be upon man's

[23] Carole Roberts, student manuscript.

sin but on the good things he has done. There was the strong
feeling that emphasis on sin would not improve the situation.
In the story or two that dealt with man's sin of a sexual nature,
the reaction was the strongest. There were strong fears of
corruption and loss of moral standards of the teen-agers by
reading such things. The desire to confine the reading to
stories about good men to inspire the youth to higher standards
of conduct was suggested on several occasions. Be that as it may,
the complaint of boredom and lack of interest was not primary
with the course. The curriculum has created more parental
interest and participation than any previously taught by this
writer. Never before have so many parents been reading their
children's assignments and discussing them around the community.

Although offensiveness cannot be the sole criterion of authen-
ticity in relation to the Christian message, history seems to bear
out the ever-present nature of this reaction when the message
of Christ is being conveyed.[24] There is no one whose faith
is not often brought to doubt by one offensive message or another from the holy Word and the corresponding offensive
experience in everyday life. The message is a "stumbling-block
to Jews and folly to Gentiles" (I Cor. 1:23). Jesus himself
experienced this: "After this many of his disciples drew back
and no longer went about with him. Jesus said to the twelve,
'Will you also go away?'" The triumph of faith is that man in
spite of the offense of the gospel sooner or later is faced with
the question of Simon Peter. "Lord, to whom shall we go?
You have the words of eternal life; and we have believed, and
have come to know, that you are the Holy One of God."
(John 6:68-69.)

Beyond the offense, the fear, the insecurity, doubt and
despair will raise a new life, a new joy, a new peace. This is

[24] Soren Kierkegaard, *The Gospel of Our Sufferings* (Grand Rapids:
Wm. B. Eerdmans Publishing Co., 1964), p. 21.

the good news of salvation, news which can only be received after one has accepted the offense which comes before. If our Christian education is to mean anything at all to our generation, it must begin leading people to experiencing Jesus as the Christ, the bearer of salvation. He is present and waiting to bring this experience in much literature and other art forms if he is only sought. The question remains whether the church of our generation will have the courage to seek this message which brings new life.

13

*Breakthrough in Burlington**

William N. Aswad

I am sure that the Chamber of Commerce of my hometown would react with mixed emotions if they were to hear me say that Burlington, Vermont, is an average American town inhabited by some thirty-five thousand average people who take much pride in their Lake Champlain, their million-dollar view of the Adirondacks, and their own Green Mountains. It is a town in which typical conversation in the summer deals with fishing, swimming, and boating. In the fall practically everyone talks deer hunting, and in the winter the big conversation is ice fishing, snow (or the lack of it), and skiing.

The point here is that aside from being blessed with a nice place to live and bring up kids, there is nothing unique or unusual about Burlington, Vermont, or the people who live there. As I said, it is an average American town with average people—statistically sixty percent Roman Catholic and forty percent Protestant.

I happen to be a member of a very small and relatively new church in Burlington which has, in its short life, received much attention across this country. Two documentary movie films have been made about this church. Its members are very frequently called to speak at retreats, seminars, men's and

* An address given at a meeting of the National Council of Churches in Louisville, Kentucky, in February, 1965.

women's groups, and other church functions around the country. Stories about this church have been written in magazines and periodicals with national circulation. I never cease to be amazed when on a business or pleasure trip to New York, Philadelphia, Los Angeles, or even a small town in the Catskills, that when the conversation gets around to church, people say to me, "Oh yes, I've heard of your church—you have a coffeehouse there." Or, "How is that church experiment going?"

There is no question in my mind that the unusual attention or recognition that this church has received can be attributed to the type of mission outreach that is expressed by the members and pastor of this church.

To be sure, people have heard of our church-sponsored coffeehouse called "The Loft." They have heard that some of our members are weekly visitors to the county jail—not as inmates! Some of our women visit with the girls in a home for unwed mothers. We have business and women's occupational groups that meet for breakfast or communion and discuss what it means to be a Christian in the secular world.

These current and other dropped or abandoned mission outreaches of this church are interesting to observe and discuss —but even they *in themselves* are not unique or unusual. Many coffeehouse missions are springing up around the country. Quite recently we heard from a seminary student who has written his thesis on "The Coffeehouse Missions."

Being concerned about unwed mothers or prisoners is not uniquely Christian, for if we look a little deeper, we find that the home for unwed mothers was founded by a nonchurch-affiliated group. Certainly there are many examples of penal reformers, legal aid societies, and other nonchurch people who have shown concern for prisoners.

What then is so different about this church and its missionary expression—if in fact it is different—that has attracted so much national attention?

For this question to be answered, it would help to review some geography and history:

The north end of Burlington is a suburban, residential area of approximately five thousand population. It is physically a peninsula of high ground almost completely surrounded by the lake, a river, and low, marsh land. The only access is a single road running north and south through this quite comfortable middle-income community.

In 1955 the Burlington Council of Churches recognized that this was a very rapidly growing community and was "unchurched" insofar as its Protestant population was concerned. By comity agreement they invited the Presbyterian Church to conduct a survey of the area and then to proceed to organize a church.

The result of that survey indicated, in the terms of the surveyors, that the area could be classed as "high potential" for new church development and that on the strength of the response and interest in the survey, any "old-line" Protestant church could be assured of becoming self-supporting in three years or less.

What happened next followed a pattern of what I am sure has been repeated and is still being followed in suburban, new church development all over the country.

A National Missions fieldworker and a representative from the presbytery assisted in bringing together neighborhood groups who were interested in forming the new church. These neighborhood groups met and selected a person from among them to serve on what was to be the organizing steering committee. The steering committee was charged with three simultaneous responsibilities and objectives. First, to expand the interest and number of participants in this project; second, to locate and procure through the presbytery a manse for the prospective pastor and land on which to build a church building; and third, to interview and assist in the selection of the pastor.

All these activities were pursued with interest, high hopes, and expectations. To be sure, there were a few obstacles and areas of uncertainty, for this embryo congregation was a rather heterogeneous group made up of Baptists, Congregationalists, Methodists, Lutherans, and five or six Presbyterians. There were even three or four ex-Roman Catholics. None of the problems at this stage were considered serious, though, and I am sure everyone felt that when the pastor arrived, he would take charge and everything would be all right.

The selection of a pastor was looked upon as an awesome task by most of the steering committee, for none had ever interviewed a minister before. It was almost predictable that the first candidate who appeared would be invited to be the pastor, for which layman among us was wise enough to pass adverse judgment on an ordained minister recommended by the presbytery?

In retrospect I have often thought that if we were to identify the turning point or the single event which has more than any other set the direction of this church, it was the calling of its pastor. As I indicated, the first candidate interviewed was invited. His response, however, both dismayed and disillusioned the committee. He stipulated that before he could accept such an offer he first must be assured of a manse for himself and his family as comfortable and large as the newly redecorated one he would be leaving. He next insisted that the committee secure in writing the names of all prospective members and the amount of money each would pledge to support the church. Since the committee was at this early stage in no position to make these guarantees or commitments, a mutaul agreement with the candidate was reached to withdraw the invitation.

The next candidate recommended by the presbytery was a newly married young man who was the son of a retired minister of a large and prominent church in a growing metropolitan area. He never had a parish of his own, but had worked in the East Harlem Protestant Parish and assisted in other project church activities.

I am sure that the committee felt that here was a young man who was ambitious and unspoiled by the experience and comforts of a well-established parish. Surely he would not put such immediate and difficult demands on us but would provide the pioneering leadership necessary to organize and build a new church. He was invited, and he accepted.

Almost simultaneously, however, and during the period between his acceptance and actual move to Burlington, the committee was busy looking for a manse to purchase and a plot of land large enough on which to build the church. Already the talk of a *building* was a subject of much interest.

The steering committee located a plot of land of approximately seven acres. On one edge of the plot stood a comfortable home and an adjoining store which sold television sets and boats. With no equity and immediate plans for a fund drive, the committee purchased the property with money from the presbytery, consisting of low interest loans and loan grants and a second mortgage from the original owner.

The new minister arrived and moved into the manse, and worship services were temporarily held in the local public school auditorium until the TV and Boat Shop could be refurbished into a chapel and church school classrooms.

What happened from this point came as a surprise to the new congregation. For the most part, I guess, they expected to participate in some brief classes before being taken into membership as a body. Some expected to be taken in with no classes at all.

It was generally expected that the new pastor would lead in the formation of a men's group, women's group, couple's club, a building committee, a fund-raising committee, membership or new life committee. People expected or looked forward to some church suppers, Christmas bazaars, white elephant sales, and all the other trivia that clutters up a church calendar. They all expected these things to some degree, depending on their previous church experience. What they got, however, was a quiet, unassuming, serious, dedicated, and consistent young man who merely asked them to come to the membership class and, with him, to examine what the church was all about and why God was calling *this particular people* together to be a part of his church universal.

Without fully realizing it at the time, this congregation was sitting down with its pastor and examining and learning, many for the first time, the nature of the ministry and who was called to do what.

Some began very early to get an inkling of this minister's concept of the ministry; others took a little longer; and some are still trying to understand him. He did not believe that he had a ministry and that we did not. He constantly sought to bring us to the realization that we are all ministers and that the only differences between us are the talents, abilities, and *primary* areas of ministry to which each of us is called. We began to learn that the terms *laymen* and *clergy* were not valid in their popular understanding. Most of the duties that we looked to the pastor to carry out, we were learning, were as much our responsibilities as his. For example, the pastor did not and does not feel that making parish calls is a duty that he alone is supposed to do. He has gently, but firmly, insisted that the elders and members of the session carry out this share of this ministry of parish calling. This emphasis on the shared ministry of the clergy and laymen has been a constant theme in this church's study, discussion, and activities.

Robert C. Johnson, who edited *The Church and Its Changing Ministry*, helps us to a better understanding of this concept. For instance, he says:

A clear example of how wrong presuppositions lead to wrong conclusions is contained in our contemporary—and inaccurate—use of the words "clergy" and "laity." Current usage, even though it is of long standing, fails to recognize that Christian ministry is the ministry of the entire body, and, therefore, it divides the Church in two, in a way that is unbiblical and debilitating. For we have forgotten that in the New Testament the words "clergy" (*kleros*, share or portion) and "laity" (*laos*, people) describe *the same persons*. The clergy are those who share the "inheritance," or those who are "in Christ" or within the Church—and this means everyone. The laity are the "people of God," or those who are "in Christ" or within the Church—and this means everyone, too. Those whom we commonly call "clergymen" are laymen, for they are among the people of God as much as anyone else. And those whom we commonly call "laymen" are clergymen, for they too, as members of the Church, share the "inheritance" as much as anyone else.

We probably find this confusing. If so, we merely share the current confusion surrounding the nature of our ministry, and merely exemplify how far all of us are from the New Testament pattern of thinking. From the moment that we transfer the responsibility for ministry to a selected or elected group, we have gone down a deadend street. For although we may be deeply concerned to *have* an effective ministry, we will necessarily forget that we have been called, one and all, to *be* the ministry of Jesus Christ. We will be unable to understand the import of the simple statement which (perhaps more accurately than any other) describes the very being of the Church: the Church *is* the ministry of Jesus Christ.[1]

As I said, this concept of the shared ministry or the ministry of the whole body has been a constant theme in the study and life of this congregation. I am not implying, however, that this approach has been accepted and understood by all. In fact,

[1] From Robert Clyde Johnson, *The Church and Its Changing Ministry*, published by the office of the General Assembly, United Presbyterian Church in the United States of America, Witherspoon Building, Philadelphia. Used by permission.

it has caused tension in the parish. We have had families transfer their membership to another church in town because the pastor did not make periodic, social calls on them. They had been used to this attention in their previous church experience and resented what they felt was a lack of concern for them.

The general subject of the duties of the pastor has been, to say the least, controversial in this church. So much so, that very recently the elders or Session of the church published the following statement on the *Responsibilities of the Pastor or Teaching Elder*. I quote:

It is our firm and unshakable conviction that the ministers of this church are its members, who are bound together in Christ, and who have promised before God to proclaim the gospel to the world in both word and deed. Accordingly, we reject the idea that any one person can be delegated this responsibility, whether such delegation is intended as that of ministry to the congregation, or that of ministry in behalf of the congregation.

We recognize, however, that as ministers we have many individual and corporate shortcomings, among which is our dismal ignorance of the Scriptures, of our sacred history, and of the many possible interpretations and implications of God's will for us. Accordingly, we have chosen to select one from among us and have instructed him to devote himself to the very specific and fulltime task of being our teacher. Our Teaching Elder has been well trained for this job, but like any other teacher, his training is never complete. We, therefore, expect that many hours of study and preparation will be required of him for every hour of teaching that we receive.

A few of the implications of this assignment of prime responsibility are worthy of note:

1. We do not consider the Teaching Elder responsible for the administration of the church and its various activities. This means that we neither expect nor desire that he devote time to prodding us, the members, into carrying out our particular responsibilities.

2. We do not consider that the Teaching Elder is responsible for

the conduct of worship services. Within the worship service itself, he has, of course, a proclaiming function to perform, and in keeping with the Constitution of the Presbyterian Church, he is responsible for the administration of the sacraments. The ultimate responsibility for the church's worship life, however, is vested solely in the Session.

3. We do not consider that the Teaching Elder is responsible for our children's religious education. Our instructions to him are that he is to concentrate his teaching on the adults of the church, as a result of which we will be better prepared as parents to teach our own children.

4. We do not consider that he has any particular responsibility for visitations to members or potential members. Calling on members, for whatever reason, is the responsibility of all the ministers of this church. We recognize, however, that the Teaching Elder is especially trained in counseling, and expect that he will continue this form of ministry in unusual circumstances, as has been his practice in the past.

The intent of this Session policy is to free our Teaching Elder from many diverse and distracting duties that are, in fact, our own responsibility, in order that he might better perform the job that we have called him here to perform. It is our sincere hope that all members of the church will join with the Session in providing the encouragement and support needed by the Teaching Elder if he is to effectively carry out his responsibility among us.

This statement on the responsibilities of the pastor, or as we chose to call him, the Teaching Elder, may be construed to be a position guide or a statement of primary work responsibilities of the pastor. I must admit, however, this position was not arrived at or developed overnight. It is the result of almost seven years of teaching, learning, discussion, debate, controversy, and prayer on the part of this parish and its pastor.

You may have noted the emphases that this statement makes are that (1) the pastor is primarily the teacher of *adults* of the congregation; and (2) he is also obviously responsible for performing a proclaiming function in the corporate worship services.

In addition to the statement adopted by the Session, the congregation has also taken hold of three words that seem to summarize their calling as a people of God. These words are *worship, study,* and *service.*

As the Session statement indicates, worship is held as a very important part of the church's life and is used as the vehicle to celebrate corporately the acts of God in the affairs of men.

The emphasis on study and specifically adult study began with the first membership classes, which lasted about six months. These adult groups continued to meet for further study in various forms over the years. A group would begin, study, and dissolve, and then another would take its place. One of the groups made up of students from the university used to meet in the pastor's living room. Out of this group grew a coffeehouse, on the campus, where students felt that they could, in their own environment, study and discuss current issues in light of the Christian faith.

From a handful of students in the pastor's living room this group grew large enough to fill an old carriage house which they rented, remodeled, and called "The Barn." Here the students felt free and uninhibited by the walls of the church or manse to hear and discuss current live issues with invited speakers and faculty and to try to discover then what God's will for them was.

The parish adult study has over the years used many books as a resource for study: the Bible, *The Church We Love* (Rowe), *Life Together* (Dietrich Bonhoeffer), *In But Not of the World* (Robert W. Spike), *I and Thou* (Martin Buber), *Man's Need and God's Action* (Reuel L. Howe), and many others.

During the past two years, however, the study has focused

on the Bible with first a complete study from Genesis to Revelation, and then a detailed study of specific chapters. During the past eight or ten months the study has concentrated on form and source criticism of the Old Testament. Recently, the emphasis has been on ethics in a Christian context and the "new humanity."

Out of the various study groups led by the Teaching Elder has grown the third emphasis of the church—that of mission. It has become obvious to the participants that study without application of the learning was an empty game and that we could not really know God's mission without being out in the world where the issues, tensions, and problems really were.

Out of one group studying the servant passages in Isaiah some men began visiting prisoners in the county jail every week. They did not go to convert anyone, or to preach, or to bring the church to the prisoners, but they went merely to be there, to hear these men, to assist with family, lawyer, or other concerns of the prisoners. This activity has led to participation in city health studies and penal reforms.

The Loft, a coffeehouse located in the heart of the business district of Burlington, grew out of an interest by two laymen who hoped to provide the city with a place where discussion, drama, art, controversial issues, and just plain good conversation and a cup of coffee could be had. The coffeehouse was later turned over to the church and is now operated by a board of directors under the Session of the church. All of the waiters, cooks, and clean-up help are volunteers and are made up of Presbyterian and other church members, including Roman Catholics, and even atheists who feel that something worthwhile is happening at The Loft.

These workers meet once a month to discuss the mechanics of running the coffeehouse, to share experiences, and to study the meaning of the servant church in the life of the community.

The Loft is also the meetingplace every Friday morning for various businessmen who gather for breakfast or communion and spend some time discussing Christian ethics in the business world, or how a Christian makes secular decisions in light of his Christian faith.

Out of the women's occupational study group grew a concern for the girls in a home for unwed mothers, known as the "Lund Home." The mission there involves just being present and concerned for the girls whose family are ashamed of them and perhaps do not visit them or those girls who feel separated from other people. It may involve bringing them to church on Sunday or providing worship in the home itself.

The most recent mission outreach is now in the discussion phase within the parish. It involves the prospect of using the land on which "the fine new church" has never been built to build a retreat or community house. This building may find use as a temporary home for prisoners newly released and looking for work. Or it may be used as a halfway house for patients seeking to move back into the life of the city. It has been suggested as an "inn" for visiting clergy, students, or new families waiting to get settled in the community. It is, finally, another attempt to put church buildings to more relevant use in God's concern for people.

I suspect that the activities of this church have come as a shock to all but one or two other churches in town. I have heard the clergy of at least one refer to us as that "fiasco out on North Avenue."

Our pastor, however, summarizes these activities in the following:

But this involvement in the affairs of the city is teaching this congregation the need for new forms of ministry, and it is making us aware of how outdated present forms and organizations are for mission in all the world. It becomes quickly apparent that parish forms must be secondary to Christ's mission; that forms are important instruments, but that *forms* of the church's life should not limit the mission, but rather assist it to go into all the corners of the world.

This means that we must allow and encourage outdated forms to die; such forms as "residential only" church patterns; nonhuman stuffy groups; "out-of-position" and "out-of-the-world" type groups.

Such groups have no right to exist in the church. We are learning that we can begin by not encouraging the existence of such groups and that, as our hands and time become more free, we are able to imagine new possibilities. The process of growth which results involves resistance and tension inside the church and confusion outside the church where people are quick to stereotype the church's movement into the world as "egghead," "beatnik," "communist," or "the girl scouts with expresso." It presents the danger of being overwhelmed by questions or criticism; but also the possibility, in the midst of it all, to witness to the gospel by clarifying the difference between the forms of the church, and the mission of God.[2]

The subjects of the "nature of the ministry" and "how to make the institutional church more relevant today" are occupying much time, thought, and discussion in the church circles. There are no easy formulas or solutions.

There is no single man-made strategy, technique, or process that will bring about the much sought-for change. But if I may be presumptuous, I might suggest that the ordained clergy themselves, at the parish level, have it within their means to at least begin the task. If each parish pastor would decide that he will no longer concern himself with the trivia which has occupied so much of his time and, instead, concentrate his energies and abilities in the activities for which he is best trained and for which he is primarily set apart, I believe that the first and maybe the major step would have been taken.

[2] Paraphrase from *"One Attempt at Ministry"* by W. H. Hollister.

The hierarchy above him, however, must then allow him the freedom and give him the support to take this step.

So many times in my business I hear that what we need is a "good organization" to get the job done. If the institutional church has anything, it does have organization. What is needed is for the organization, in all its power and resources, to begin to concentrate on what is important and to give support and assistance to the local parish where the signs of the new humanity and the coming of the kingdom are to be found.

In closing, let me share with you another statement adopted by the Session of the church, in 1963, in Burlington. This is a concise statement which sets the direction for this church.

We believe that God is at work in the world today in many ways and in many places. He actually came into the world in the human form of Jesus Christ as proof of his love for mankind; and, through Christ's life, death, and resurrection, we know that his mission in the world will continue until the kingdom is complete. We believe it to be the primary job of the church to seek where God is at work and to follow him there in obedient service.

We believe that God is at work in Burlington. He is in our homes, our places of work, our jail, our courts, our city hall, our slums, our playgrounds, our schools, and our churches. He is at work in urban renewal, reapportionment, race relations, and wherever there is social tension. And, we believe that Christ Church, Presbyterian, exists in order to join God in his work in Burlington and beyond. To this end, we must boldly set a course of action that will enable us to be where he would have us be, and to do there what he would have us do.

We believe that parish organization and activity must be consistent with and supportive to this church's purpose. It must be flexible and responsive to the ever-changing location and nature of God's work in the community. And it must be free to change, open to criticism, and willing to fail.

We believe that faithfulness to God is the only criterion by which we can make our decisions.

14

New Ministries of the Church

R. Edward Dowdy

There are no "new" ministries of the church. At least we have not found them at Woodruff Place Baptist Church in Indianapolis. Whenever we think we have hit on some new need or come up with some novel way to become involved in the lives of the people in our community, we are sure to find that it has been done before. A little search of church history, a deeper study of the New Testament invariably reveal that what we thought was new is not new at all, for "there is nothing new under the sun."

Several years ago Dr. Clarence Cranford said, "Whenever a new book comes out, I read an old one." We who are trying to minister in the inner city profit greatly by reading an old Book. It deals with the life and ministry of one "who went about doing good."

When we started the Mother's Club recently, we thought we were rising to a newly felt need in our community. There are young mothers almost too young to be mothers but who desperately need to know about rearing a family. Others are so disadvantaged educationally that they cannot read the labels in the supermarket to know which is the best buy in terms of size and price. They are forever misled by SPECIAL 10¢ OFF REGULAR PRICE and oversize boxes that say GIANT, ECONOMY, or FAMILY SIZE, but when the cost per ounce is calculated, it is a better buy to get the regular size.

In order to get the mothers together some provision had to be made for child care during the meetings each Friday morning. Sponsored by ours and a neighbor church, the Mother's Club has been unusually popular and fruitful from its inception. We might claim a "first" if we neglected to remember the words of a certain man of Galilee who said to his disciples, "Let the children come unto me, and do not hinder them; for to such belongs the kingdom of God." Their mothers had brought the children for Jesus to bless; he welcomed their concern for their children and took advantage of it. Parents today are anxious to do everything for their children; we simply capitalize on this natural desire.

When the women in a Sunday school class determined to do something for a family whose welfare check is used up paying the rent, they decided to provide supplemental food for the blind couple. This couple is not really "our responsibility," for after all, they are not even Baptist. Actually they are not "our kind of people," for they are "welfare folk," and we are an average middle-class church. Our women determined that the need was real, and they provided staple foods from their own pantries so that there is available at the church a supply of the basic necessities. They thought they had hit on something new until they recalled the words of Jesus, "I was hungry and you gave me food. . . . As you did it to one of the least of these my brethren, you did it to me."

I shall never forget the absolute joy which was expressed when we hit on the idea of sending out our visitors two by two to call in the apartments of people who had some tenuous connection with our church. One deacon reasoned, "It would be safer at night to go in pairs. If one person runs out of something to talk about, surely the other can think of something to say. It *is* harder to say 'No' to two people than it would be to say 'No' to a person alone."

Perhaps they had forgotten the example of Jesus as he sent

his disciples out to visit two by two. We used the same technique of sending the callers to the home of the most likely prospects the first night. Having found some success, with renewed confidence, then they were ready for the less-willing-to-listen group. This technique was not invented by the modern evangelists; we simply followed Christ's example of good judgement.

The kids in our neighborhood have no place to play except the narrow, busy streets. Ten years ago we paved two city lots for a parking lot. The space was needed for Sunday and other times when cars of church members would be crowding the available street parking space. Although our immediate neighborhood is not exactly a high-income area, the people seem to have a lot of cars per family.

We determined that the parking lot would be used for a playground except when it was absolutely needed for church parking. We made a ten-foot-square sandbox and erected a jungle gym, made of scrap pipe. It seemed like a new idea at the time, but then I read that half a century ago, Walter Rauschenbusch was advocating a sandbox for each of the New York city playgrounds. This was long before the teachers of young children discovered the learning value of "mud therapy." Our kids were getting dirty enough, but the wet sand gave them a new opportunity to be creative in their play.

On that same concrete "playground" which is only eighty by one hundred feet, we have done many things. Last summer we staged neighborhood Olympic games with our Presbyterian neighbors. Discus throwing with paper plates and shot putting with a balloon would provide poor preparation for the real Olympics, but the Woodruff Place laurel crown was just as proudly worn.

One year, we took advantage of the best-known event in sporting, the Indianapolis "Five Hundred" which comes every Memorial Day. On our parking lot we painted an oval track and announced the coming of the Woodruff Place "Little Five Hundred." Competition was open to all ages. It was to be, as the real Five Hundred is, an endurance race. Speed did not count. The idea was to complete five hundred laps around the oval track. After a twenty-five-lap "qualifying" run, the laps could be done in multiples of twenty-five at the contestant's convenience. Judges and timers for the big event consisted of "anyone who can count up to twenty-five." A more conscientious group of six- and seven-year-old officials you never saw! The parking lot is lighted at night, so the track was in use from early morning till late at night.

The rules specified that any type of vehicle could be used in the Woodruff Place "Little Five Hundred." Contestants made their five hundred laps on bicycles, roller skates, pushing baby carriages, rolling an automobile tire, or just plain running. The official score cards were a bit grimy when they were turned in with very juvenile signatures, certifying that each twenty-five laps had been logged. Some barely held together in a sweaty hip pocket until the contest was completed. Watermelon for the winners in "victory lane" was promptly followed by enough watermelon for all who were standing by to cheer the winners.

We simply took advantage of a local interest in a five hundred mile race. The children loved it. We had a feeling it would not have been strange to the man of Galilee who had observed children in the streets playing wedding or funeral in typical imitation of their elders.

The census figures indicate a higher than usual number of older people in our neighborhood. What could be more natural than a "Golden Age" club? It took so little doing to get the group together that we wondered why we had not tried it earlier. We already had several Sunday school classes and women's circles for older women, and the Men's Bible Class. Our weekly Golden Age Fellowship fulfills quite a different need for people who spend most of their time alone or in the home of a relative. One of our octogenarians said that he felt "completely rejuvenated" by the afternoon spent with the Golden Age Fellowship. They have a wonderful time playing games like dominoes and scrabble.They have some favorite television programs to share. A group of ladies often spends the whole day working on a quilt and talking. We think the talking is just as important as the games and the quilting. Then there is refreshment time. A cake with candles occasionally helps the group to celebrate with one who might be passing another birthday alone. Even the diabetics are not forgotten, and there is always something tasty that contains no sugar.

Some may question whether or not this is a "religious" activity. We think it is in the best tradition of the one who said something about "a cup of cold water." Of course it is religious in a traditional way too when a retired minister thanks God for the food and the fellowship. The selection of movies includes some of religious content, but none are more religious, in fact, than the beautiful travel pictures that reveal God's wonders of creation. A trip to a farm, or to a state park when the autumnal beauty of colored leaves is at its peak—this too speaks of our God who cares.

The Golden Age Thanksgiving dinner is a real "event." The turkey is cooked by a retired construction contractor. He has been doing the family cooking since he terminated his building work at ninety. He tested several receipts for turkey dressing before he was satisfied he had found the best formula for the Golden Age version. No dinner at the White House gets more careful preparation than our Golden Age Thanksgiving.

We had an idea that our neighborhood mothers needed some home nursing training. We always have lots of kids with measles and mumps. There are grandparents who are bedfast.

Scarcely a day goes by without a need for some first-aid experience.

Our first effort was a complete failure. The mothers did not come. We thought we had failed to convince them of the need, but it was really a matter of time. We had nearly perfect response when we scheduled the same course for the Girl Scouts and invited other teen-age girls to share. They are the baby-sitters' and it is this age group who are most involved in caring for grandma. Sponge baths, backrests made from cardboard boxes, and other home nursing techniques were teen-age concerns.

For four years our church has operated basketball leagues in our gym which was the first gymnasium in our part of town. Dr. L. C. Trent, who was pastor when the gym was built, called it the "evangelistic doorway to the church." He had a conviction that if the men could get boys into the building, he could teach them the way of Christ. We have been teaching a lot more than basketball across the years. Obviously, we have not made saints out of all who have come to play. Some never do more than just play the game. Others are enlisted in the other youth activities of the church. Some get only a chance to be related to a Christian coach who is concerned about each boy as a person. Somebody cares when a boy has a problem. When he goes to Juvenile Court, it says something of the love of Christ just to have someone from the church standing with him or sitting with his estranged parents.

We have convictions that a cooperative nursery school has real value for both children and parents. The public school kindergarten teachers have assured us that they can immediately spot a new pupil who has had the nursery school experience. They have already learned to share. They know better how to get along with other children. They have already been trained to leave parents and accept the teacher as friend and mentor.

Ours is not a day nursery but a cooperative one. It serves

the needs of parents who must work all day and leave the children from early morning until the end of the workday. Our cooperative is specifically designed to involve each parent in the role of a "helping parent" on a shared basis and also provides for parent education in regular monthly sessions. From the employed, trained teacher, both child and parent learn. Within the parents' group, the sharing is itself very creative and comforting. Just to know that other parents are having the same kind of experiences in child rearing saves inexperienced parents from panic and discouragement.

We had not planned it this way, but an extra opportunity came to us from one of our local hospitals. A preschool child who was under psychiatric care was enrolled by the hospital. The doctors thought he would respond to being in a group of so-called normal children. A trained caseworker came with him each day, and both were quickly accepted in the nursery school group. We felt that everyone profited from the experience.

In other instances, welfare and community agencies have been sending young people and adults to us because they recognize the basic needs which the church is fulfilling. A teen-age girl who has spent many months in the hospital for corrective surgery came to us on such a recommendation. Our youth group immediately welcomed her. In a short time she started to share in the leadership of the group. After a few months she was as much at home as though she had grown up in the church. We remember the first night after a basketball game, when she said, "This is the first time in my life that I have had any fun."

A boy on probation from the Juvenile Court needed a friend. He had broken no law, but a series of unfortunate circumstances at home had put him into court. Because we had shown interest in some of our own boys who were before the court at the same time, the probation officer asked if we would be willing to add a new boy to our responsibility. Several years later, after finishing high school and a tour duty in the Marines, this "predelinquent" came by to say, "Thanks for keeping me off the streets."

Our study hall and tutoring sessions have not completely solved the dropout problem, but these have helped. A place to study with some books and a qualified teacher to help has proved its worth. When the high-school invitations for commencement came in last year, there was one from a near-dropout who was literally saved from suicide by an alert tutor who thought he detected evidences of too much medication.

Whatever "new ministries" we have been able to engage in are largely the results of church members' giving more of their time and talent to share in a work that belongs to the whole church and not to staff only. We have been aided by college and seminary interns, who worked many hours a week for a bare subsistence and the joy of working. Two summers we have had high-school young people whose home church paid their expenses so they could help us. The Indiana Baptist Youth Fellowship provided a summer scholarship for another. Actually the amount of money involved was small, but having a little extra help made the difference of doing or not doing some immediate project.

The American Baptist Home Mission Society helped by sending a staff person to aid in our training for the winter volunteers. Members from suburban churches served as helpers, taught piano lessons, and provided transportation for field trips. The Neighborhood Youth Corps has even asked us to provide employment for high-school young people who are working under the Economic Opportunity Act. We have been very fortunate in having an abundance of manpower available. Perhaps there is a contagion that grows out of work that is so rewarding, whether as volunteers, interns, or subsistence workers.

There is really nothing "new" about what we have been

doing. It just seems appropriate to try to meet the needs of people, whatever those needs happen to be. This is our understanding of what Jesus did whenever he confronted a person in trouble.

"Truly, truly, I say to you, he who believes in me will also do the works that I do; and greater works than these will he do, because I go to the Father." (John 14:12.)

15

Encounter—Adults and the Gospel

Paul R. Long, Jr.

The problem is a simple one; it has to do with effectively communicating the gospel, the "good news" that God was in Christ reconciling the world to himself. There are obviously many schools of thought about the effective communication of the gospel. At Third Church in Rochester we have embarked on a program that has to do with "dialogue." It is concerned with the dispersed church reaching out into the community for nurture and action. Through this program we are attempting to establish a community of searching Christians who need one another to witness to a living and relevant, yet historically sound, Christian faith. In order for the gospel to be authentically proclaimed, the listeners must become hearers; the listeners must be involved in the proclamation; the listeners must be able to ask questions and to press on toward deeper meanings and must be allowed to "get hold of" the proclaimers.

At Third Church this is an evolving and vital program. Basic to it is an exchange of ideas and concerns about some of the "basic words" of Christianity. The opportunity for this exchange is made available through the gathering together of *short-term, disciplined,* small groups meeting in the home of the minister of adult education. These are not koinonia groups but are merely the beginning attempt in communication of ideas that have always been a part of the Christian vocabulary. The groups are short-term. This means that they have a beginning and an ending. How many of us have been involved in those groups that go on and on and if our resistance is high, how often are we involved in endless discussion concerning whether we should go on or not, and how often are loyalties tested by the ability of a person to put up with something that has fulfilled its usefulness? Thus, the groups are short-term—six weekly meetings, the dates presented as a part of the call to meeting. The group members agree to accept a minimal but important *discipline*: The individual meetings begin at 8 P.M. with a social hour; the discussion period begins at 8:30 P.M. sharp; and the discussion period ends promptly at 10 P.M. The groups are small. We will not convene if we do not have at least twelve people, and we limit the group to eighteen. Notices are released through the church newsletter, and interested people sign up in the church office. If we do not have twelve participants one week before the first meeting, we postpone the first meeting for two weeks. If we do not have our twelve one week before the new meeting night, we cancel the group. The size of the group is important, and with the fifteen groups we have had over the last eighteen months, we have found that the Basic Word Group works better with eighteen people. This is large enough to hide within but small enough to allow everybody the opportunity to speak. The group leader (the minister of adult education) encourages all to participate, but it is also his task to protect those who are not ready to become actively involved. After all, and this is important, this is a "basic" course with more to follow, and conversation, true and honest dialogue, can be very threatening to many people.

The "basic words" discussed in this program are faith, grace, sin, salvation, Christmas, and Easter. There is no assigned reading; participants may read anything they like, but they may not quote extensively from books or other authority figures. Hopefully, this is an opportunity to dredge up some of the insights or lack of insights that each person has within him. The minister of adult education begins each session with, "The basic word for tonight is. . . ." He is then quiet for at least the first half of the meeting, and actually his role is of moderator and discussion leader rather than that of resource person. The general atmosphere of this series is geared toward "search" rather than "find." After all, there is more to come.

At the close of the six meetings the group dissolves. There will be rumblings like, "We are only just getting to know each other" or "We have just scratched the surface," and while this is true, we keep the discipline and dissolve the group as originally planned. Those who have completed it are eligible to become involved in the second phase of our evolving program, and this offer is made clear.

At this point in the life of Third Church the second phase has two aspects. The first is Contract Groups. A topic is chosen by the minister of adult education and is publicized as a possible relevant discussion subject. Those interested are encouraged to sign up to convene and discuss the possibilities of such a topic. The number in this group is not as important as the larger groups, although we have found that a minimum of eight and a maximum of sixteen seem to work best. The group decides its own contract, number of meetings, how often the meetings are held, the books to be read, and so forth. In this kind of group the minister assumes a new role as a participant in the group and a resource person. He is important at the convening meeting particularly. At this time he suggests the number of meetings (six works out best still), how often the group should meet (every week is still best, following the Basic Word format although we have had Contract groups that have met every other week), and the books to be read. If the minister instigates the topic, a list of readings is sent out before the convening meeting so that the participants know what is required. Also, it is up to the minister to determine the format of the discussion period either by doing this himself or by encouraging one of the other participants to do it. If a book is our "authority," we do not read it chapter by chapter but attempt to deal with its major points after every member has read it. On this basis with the minister as instigator, groups in Third Church have studied Saul Alinsky and the Industrial Areas Foundation, leading into the book *Crisis in Black and White* by Charles Silberman. There have been groups on Bible study, drama (*The Deputy*), and politics. An important phase of this Contract Group program is the action that might follow the period of study on a particular topic. An action project is presented, and the group is encouraged to consider it as a possible reason to continue beyond its agreed upon number of meetings. In the case of the Saul Alinsky group, action was very important, and this group of twelve laymen was instrumental in the invitation to bring the Industrial Areas Foundation to Rochester. The group continued to meet for about one year on a weekly basis and now has become absorbed into the various aspects of Rochester community organization. However, the minister is important as a dissolver, and in Third Church five groups have been dissolved at the close of their study period.

There is developing within Third Church a group consciousness, and this seems to be the "growing edge" of this phase of our program. In October 1965 a Basic Word graduate called and asked that a Contract Group be formed around the general topic, "How to Communicate an Authentic Sex Ethic to Teen-Agers." I suggested that this person gather together a group of Basic Word graduates to form a Contract Group on this topic. This was done, and we have been meeting with James Pike's book, *Teen-Agers and Sex,* as the authority. This group is made up of sixteen parents (couples) of teen-agers and meets every week for six weeks—an exciting development in our Contract Group program. Another is the drawing together of eight groups to be involved in a housing rehabilitation program in the city of Rochester. Most of these people are Basic Word graduates, and a part of the program is to involve them in a meaningful understanding of the "Church in the City." Both the sex and housing study groups were begun out of lay concern and moved through this new, small group vehicle. We now have the means through which the concerned layman can begin to enter into dialogue with the gospel on his terms and through his concerns.

The second aspect of our small group program is Secondary Study Groups, and here we are venturing into the possibilities and dangers of the church within the church. Graduates of Basic Word Groups are drawn together for a retreat experience to begin to see if the demands of the gospel can be met in the twentieth century. The initial meeting is an all-day one, and the language and social barriers that separate us are attacked. After the initial encounter the group moves into a study of parts of *The Cost of Discipleship* by Dietrich Bonhoeffer. This group meets for a definite number of meetings—usually six and usually every other week. During the series a number of action projects are presented, and as the group considers the demands of Christ as communicated by Bonhöffer, the possibilities of a continued relationship toward the renewal of the church are pursued. The minister-teacher must be a member of this group and must be continually ready to interpret the importance of both the inclusive and exclusive church. At the sixth meeting the group decides if it should continue and try to meet the demands of the gospel as a group within the institutional church.

Other phases of our program have to do with promoting the idea of conversation. Basic Words falls into this category as do the "briefing" meetings in which issues of concern are presented at luncheon, as well as a series of luncheon meetings for men and women within the industrial and home sphere.

I would say that there is an exciting awareness of the value of the Christian community evolving. While the minister's presence is essential in the preliminary stages, I have begun to sense that the layman is able and willing to join with other laymen to proclaim the gospel. The groundwork must obviously be laid, and the minister must be continually available as a guide and consultant. Within this church the possibilities are unlimited.

16

Ministry in High-Rise Apartments

David C. Rich

Picture, for a moment, two identical high-rise luxury apartment buildings, each twenty-one stories high, each with 560 apartments ranging from studio to three-bedroom units. Doormen stand protectively at each entrance. Play areas for children are adjacent to each building with a convenient shopping center stretching alongside. Underground there is a garage for three hundred automobiles.

The pastor of the Protestant church across the street watches with anticipation the rise from rubble of these sleek concrete cobwebs of windows which will be home to two thousand men, women, and children. Surely, this will mean new life for his struggling parish.

As people move into the buildings, he organizes teams of carefully trained laymen to knock on all 560 doors in each building to welcome the new neighbors and to subtly mention the little church across the street. It takes several weeks to accomplish this task, but he feels that it is worth the effort. But alas, no one comes to the church from the new buildings.

Realizing that a different approach is needed, the minister engages a public relations firm to write the "perfect" letter of welcome to the neighborhood expressing the church's willingness to help in any way. It is sent to all 1,120 apartments, but only one person comes to the church because of the letter.

Needless to say, he is a discouraged and dismayed minister. Such was the experience of one minister and church in New York City in their attempt to minister to high-rise apartment dwellers.

For the past three years the Madison Avenue Baptist Church in New York City has been involved in an experimental apartment house ministry. Located at the corner of Madison Avenue and Thirty-First Street for over one hundred years, the church has seen its neighborhood shift from a fashionable community of mansions and expansive lawns to a commercial complex of wholesale furniture showrooms and ladies' undergarment factories. Living quarters in the immediate vicinity of the church are limited to several apartment hotels built in the 1920's, a few walk-up brownstones, and two or three old-style apartment buildings.

Nevertheless, as one moves east from the church toward the East River, one begins to encounter new high-rise apartment buildings built in the last ten years between First and Third Avenues. Old brownstones in that area are being gutted out and renovated. Tenaments are being razed for a city-administered housing project as well as for privately financed middle-income apartment buildings. It is an area in transition from the old to the new in housing.

Under the leadership of the Reverend John Saunders Bone, the pastor of Madison Avenue Baptist Church since 1959, members of the church began to ask what the relationship was of Madison Avenue Church to these fast rising buildings. What was the church's ministry to the many thousands who lived in these concrete cubicles, and what form should it take?

Concerned with these questions, the members voted to add a Minister of Community Services to its staff for three years whose responsibility, among others, would be experimentation in an apartment house ministry. In the summer of 1963 my family and I came to Madison Avenue Baptist Church and moved into a three-room apartment in Kips Bay Plaza, located between First and Second Avenues and Thirtieth and Thirty-Third Streets, nine blocks south of the United Nations and directly opposite the New York University-Bellevue Medical Center. Privately financed, Kips Bay Plaza is owned and managed by Alcoa Residences, Inc., an affiliate of the Aluminum Company of America.

Knowing that firsthand knowledge was needed, we attempted to get "the feel" of apartment house living during our first year. What is it like to live with two thousand neighbors? What are the problems encountered? What is the apartment dweller like? Because of the negative experiences of other ministers and churches we did not try any mass mailings to tenants, nor did we go around knocking on doors. Instead, we met people casually in the laundry room, on the playground, at the mailbox, and in the lobby. Acquaintances developed into friendships, and we were able to notice several characteristics about the apartment dweller.

First, he seeks anonymity and privacy. In a world of committees, jangling telephones, and ever-present people in subways, buses, elevators, stores, and on the streets, the apartment becomes the place to be alone or to be with his family. It is the retreat—the haven away from the hustle and bustle of the city. It is the place to read, to think, to gain perspective, to entertain his friends. It is the place in which to be himself. He seeks privacy because he needs privacy in the midst of a city of people, and because he seeks privacy, he respects the privacy of his neighbors. He does not want to get involved with them. There is very little "over-the-back-fence" camaraderie in an apartment building.

Second, he is mobile. There is a residential mobility as well as a job mobility, for the apartment building is a stopping-off place to the suburbs. It is a transient place. Most tenants sign for short-term leases—one to three years—for they know there

171

is a good chance that either they will be transferred to the Atlanta office or the second baby will push them further into the suburbs.

Third, he is supicious of institutions. Because of his mobility, he does not want to get involved in institutional structures and activities such as the church, the synagogue, or other forms of organized life. Such organizations represent permanence to the apartment dweller, and as a person on the move, he does not want anything that might tie him down. Also, some persons have been hurt by bad experiences with organizations. One person in our apartment building put it this way: "I was used by my church back home, running from this meeting to that meeting, and I don't want it to happen again."

Fourth, he is a person without roots. Although he may live in a New York apartment, his roots are not there. Roots, if there are any, are back home—in Boston, Des Moines, or Birmingham. Christmas, Easter, and most weekends bring on an exodus from the city as the mobile apartment dweller leaves for the beach, the country, or a visit with folks or friends "back home."

What then is the ministry of the church to such a person? For some churches the only reason to be involved with apartment buildings and the tenants who live within them is recruitment—to maneuver people into the pews.

At Madison Avenue Church we understood the mission of God in the world as a ministry of reconciliation, and our church was called to be an agent of reconciliation. The ministry was not recruitment; it was reconciliation. As an agent of reconciliation, the church seeks to break down the barriers and walls that divide us as nations, people, and as persons; it responds to the social, political, educational, cultural, and personal needs of people, and it places these needs and concerns before the needs and wants of the local church.

But how is such a ministry of reconciliation expressed to the high-rise dweller? What must the church do to perform such a task? Traditionally, the marks of the church have been the Word rightly preached and the sacraments properly administered. Today, however, writes Dr. James B. Ashbrook of the Colgate Rochester Divinity School, we must add a third mark of the church dialogue:

> Dialogue or open-faced discussion as a third mark of the faithful church points toward a new style of ministry. Our Lord reminds us of that which is everywhere possible yet seldom actual. Where two or three are gathered together in his name, there he is in their midst. Where two or three are gathered together in a power of a caring concern that stands under each person's personal sharing —there is meaning in their midst. Physical presence with personal sharing—a condition that does not guarantee the living Word, but a condition that prepares the way.[1]

Dr. Ashbrook points to the key for an appropriate and meaningful apartment house ministry—"physical presence with personal sharing." In the midst of an apartment house complex made up of the old and the young, the anonymous and the lonely, the mobile and the uprooted, there is need for personal sharing and communication among persons. There is need for persons to share life together—to meet, to talk, to share common concerns and interests so that the barriers which often divide us can be broken down. With such a concern in mind my wife and I decided to form several small interest groups in which persons could choose to participate for a short period of time.

The first group was a playreading-discussion group. A notice was placed on the bulletin board outside the laundry room asking if persons were interested in reading and discussing some contemporary plays. Ten persons responded, including a managing editor of a sports magazine, a drama student, a

[1] Sermon by Dr. James B. Ashbrook preached in the Brick Presbyterian Church, Rochester, New York, on Sunday, October 31, 1965.

set designer for theater productions, a credit manager, and several wives. It was decided that we would meet once a month in different apartments to read such plays as *JB* by Archibald MacLeish, *The Cocktail Party* by T. S. Eliot, *The American Dream* by Edward Albee, *Cat on a Hot Tin Roof* by Tennessee Williams, and others. No attempt was made to talk about the Christian faith although all who were involved knew that I was a minister. Discussion was spirited as the plays raised very real questions about life and its meaning, about love, relationships, motivations, and such. So the plays helped us focus on our own questions and needs.

A second apartment house group was organized around the "Great Decisions—1965" study program sponsored by the Foreign Policy Association. This is an eight-week study program in which persons engage in the study and discussion of issues facing the United States in the field of foreign policy. Again the approach was the same—a notice was placed on the bulletin board, and twelve persons responded. We began meeting on Monday evenings with the participants including a psychologist, a ballet instructor for children, a secretary, a bus driver, a doctor, and several wives. Discussion was again quite spirited with a variety of opinions represented. At the conclusion of the eight weeks several members of the group suggested that we continue to meet using a different study book. The psychologist suggested a paperback edited by Dr. Rollo May, *Existential Psychology*, which we read and discussed during the spring months.

With the reading of this book, the participants began to "jell" as a group, for we found ourselves moving from the rather safe discussion of political crisis "out there" to a sharing of questions and concerns about ourselves. As we moved further into May's book, persons began to share their own needs with the group. Barriers were broken down, and we listened patiently as one person talked of the problems of being single in New

York and a widow related her efforts to bring up two teen-agers without a father. The atmosphere was one of openness and honesty in which we attempted to listen to one another and to take one another seriously.

During the summer months we did not meet, but we resumed our Monday meetings in the fall with Harvey Cox's *Secular City* as the basis of our discussion and sharing. While reading this book, the group participated in a "Life in the City" conversation held at Madison Avenue Baptist Church with church members in which there was opportunity to focus together on our common life in the city.

At the conclusion of the discussion of Cox's book I asked the group to talk about our year together. What had it meant to them? Why did they come? Their response can be summed up in the words of several of the participants.

"At first I came because I enjoyed the discussion. It was spirited, and I enjoyed the interplay of ideas among various people, but after awhile I noticed that there was more to these meetings than the discussion, for I felt a commitment to the group—a concern for the group and for individuals with the group."

Another person admitted that at one point during the year she had dropped out because she was uncomfortable about some of the ideas that were being expressed. "They were too liberal for me. But after missing several of the Monday meetings I found that I missed the group, for here was a group that was willing to take me seriously even though the people disagreed with me. And I came back because of that concern."

Finally, another person mentioned that because of the openness and the honesty among the persons within the group, "I found that I could be more open and more honest with the people I work with."

Such statements recall the words of Paul Tillich in his sermon *The New Being*:

Where one is grasped by a human face as human, although one has to overcome personal distaste, or racial strangeness, or national conflicts, or the differences of sex, of age, of beauty, of strength, of knowledge, and all the other innumerable causes of separation —*there* New Creation happens! Mankind lives because this happens again and again. And if the Church which is the assembly of God has an ultimate significance, this is its significance: That here the reunion of man to man is pronounced and confessed and realized, even if in fragments and weaknesses and distortions. The Church is the place where the reunion of man with man is an actual event.[2]

Here were four Jews, one Roman Catholic, and five Protestants experiencing the "reunion of man with man as an actual event." Here were ten persons (only three went to church or to the synagogue with any regularity) meeting together and sharing life together. Here was physical presence with personal sharing. Here was the church serving as an agent of reconciliation.

This is our beginning with an apartment house ministry. It was limited, and only one person joined Madison Avenue Church because of this ministry. Nevertheless, we see the ministry to the high-rise dweller not in terms of recruitment but in terms of reconciliation—the breaking down of barriers that divide person from person. Our ministry is to combine physical presence with personal sharing in the midst of a high-rise apartment building.

Out of this experiment we see emerging three basic guidelines for an apartment house ministry.

First, the church must take the apartment house dweller seriously. Because of his need for privacy, his mobility, his rootlessness, his distrust of institutional busywork, the apartment dweller often does not find the traditional program of the church very meaningful. It does not meet his needs. Therefore, the

[2] Paul Tillich, *The New Being* (New York: Charles Scribner's Sons, 1955), p. 23.

church must shape its ministry to the dweller at his point of interest and concern rather than to try to involve him in a pre-planned structure or program.

Second, the church as an agent of reconciliation must be willing to go where people are living—go where people are, for they cannot be expected to come to the church. One reason for the effectiveness of the groups in Kips Bay is that they met where people lived and not in the church recreation hall. The church must leave the institutional walls so that the apartment dweller begins to see the church not as the building on the corner but as the people who meet on Monday evenings in apartment 1-A. For this task laity must be trained to serve as catalytic agents of reconciliation in order to develop groups within the apartment buildings.

Third, the church must meet people around a common need or interest. Our booming population presents certain challenges. It is creating people without roots—people living in constant transition. Therefore, there is real need for small group involvement in which people can meet to share life together. Such involvement might take the form of (1) groups that center in the concerns of work, (2) groups that meet to discuss common issues of the world—poverty, housing, racial differences, (3) groups that meet around community problems, housing, or school issues, or (4) groups that discuss the meaning of life in relationship to film and drama and the arts.

As an agent of reconciliation, the church is called to a servant ministry in God's world. Such a servant ministry calls us to be concerned for people where they work and play and live. In the midst of the increasing number of high-rise apartments springing up in the urban and suburban areas of our nation, the church is called to be present: "For where two or three are gathered in my name, there am I in the midst of them." Such is the task of the church in its ministry to the high-rise apartment dweller.

17

Dialogue in Goshen

Raymond C. Phibbs

That the Church of Christ, Congregational, in Goshen, Connecticut, should be written about in a book entitled *The Church Creative* will strike many Goshenites as funny. A book on "The Church Average" or "The Church Struggling" would seem to be a more appropriate place to tell the story of our church's life. Most Goshen folks would say that there are only two things that distinguish Goshen from a thousand other little towns: It is the highest and coldest community in Connecticut, and we have had in our 225-year history one great moment of glory. In 1819 the first missionaries to the Hawaiian Islands were ordained and commissioned in our church because it was the first church in America to request that a Christian mission be opened in the islands of the Pacific.

That was a glorious and creative moment in the life of our church. But that was almost 150 years ago. What about now? Well, we see ourselves as pretty average. Like so many other churches, our attendance at worship is nothing to brag about. Our economic reach seems always to exceed our grasp so that each year we fall just a little short of reaching our proposed budget. We get enough money to keep going, and even growing, but we are always left after our annual November Christian Enlistment with the certain knowledge that we could have done better.

We say with some justification that it is more than geography that puts Goshen's two churches at the center of our community. In a real sense, the churches remain the heart of this little town. Yet, we are made aware daily of the failure of the church to meet the needs of our community. While the number of problems in family living is probably no greater in Goshen than in other towns, there are enough of them to make us realize how inadequate our ministry is to our families. We are aware that the organizational life of our church often contributes to the fragmentation of family life, that there is resentment created by the demands of the church that puts additional strain on family relations, and that we have as yet found no solution to the problem our church has created. We are aware also that many men—perhaps most—in Goshen find little if any meaning in the life of the church and that it is as true of us as of most other churches that while we provide some sort of helpful ministry to the women and the children where they live, we give little to the men in the place where they must live.

So, in Goshen the church has failed to win the commitment and concern of many Goshen residents, and we fail so often to meet the needs of the persons who are committed to and involved in this life.

I have given this recital of our church's failing not because I am overburdened with a sense of failure and frustration. I am not. I recite our failures only to provide the proper perspective for the understanding of what is happening among us now.

By the grace of God, in spite of our weakness and failure, there is a new thing being done among us. By the power of the Holy Spirit, the wall of hostility and indifference that has separated Christians in Goshen is beginning to be torn down, and a bridge of mutual understanding and concern is being built over the gulf that separates Catholic Christians from Protestant Christians, and together Catholic and Protestant Christians are beginning to reach out in concern to their Jewish brothers.

There are only two churches in Goshen—our church and St. Thomas of Villanova Roman Catholic Church, with the great majority of Goshen's fourteen hundred residents about equally divided between them. Catholic and Protestant neighbors got along famously as they worked together in the Goshen Players, the Goshen Fair, the Grange, PTO, and other civic activities. However, in order to assure such harmony we all had to ignore graciously the fact that we all belong to two churches that did not get along very well. The prevailing attitude was, "You go to your church, and I'll go to mine." No one ever said, so far as we know, "You do it your way, and I'll do it God's way."

Nevertheless, what few of us saw as necessary and some thought undesirable began to happen anyway. In April, 1963, Father William J. Riley came to Goshen as the new pastor of St. Thomas Church. My wife and I invited him up to the parsonage for lunch one day shortly after he arrived, and as we talked over soup and sandwiches, we discovered that both of us had very much on our minds the problem of the renewal of Christ's church and the development of a relevant ministry to the modern world. We agreed that the church needed to make some very real changes in its life and practices if it was to do what its Lord would have it do in our day. During the course of our conversation we began to talk of the weakness that is created by the division among Christians. From facing this sad fact, we had the idea of getting our two churches together in some sort of dialogue in order to express whatever unity there is in Christ's church and to explore the possibilities of better understanding and closer cooperation between Goshen's two churches.

On the last Sunday of October, 1963—Reformation Day for Protestants and the Feast of Christ Our King for Catholics—

we scheduled an ecumenical dinner and dialogue in the local American Legion Hall. Over three hundred persons, almost evenly divided between Catholic and Protestant, attended the potluck dinner and remained for the after dinner program. Father Kevin Lynch, associate editor of *The Ecumenist* magazine, and Dr. Robert Paul, professor of church history at Hartford Seminary Foundation and former World Council of Churches executive, spoke on recent ecumenical developments in the Catholic and Protestant churches. There was much interest and excitement among members of both churches, and before the evening was over, we had agreed to schedule a Week of Prayer for Christian Unity in January.

In January, 1964, we scheduled a second ecumenical dialogue, this time in the sanctuary of our church, with Father Lynch and Dr. Paul again our guest leaders. Some two hundred persons, again almost evenly divided between Catholic and Protestant (this equal division was held in almost all subsequent meetings, whether large or small), heard Dr. Paul and Father Lynch discuss the New Testament understanding of the church. It is safe to say that while most of those present felt that the discussion was often over their heads, they wanted to see the dialogue continued in some, perhaps more comprehensible, form.

During the remaining six evenings of that week we scheduled brief, identical services of prayer for Christian unity in the two churches. The attendance each evening was gratifyingly large. We gathered, each in his own church, and prayed for each other. We could be in one accord in our prayers for each other, but we could not yet be in one place to express that accord. We could be united in prayer, but we had to be separated in order to offer those prayers.

From these beginnings, initiated by Father Riley and myself, the dialogue began to take root in our town, and others began to create occasions for its expression. The Pilgrim Fellowship of our church and the Catholic Youth Organization of St. Thomas Church carried on for one year a joint youth ministry in a neighboring state hospital. On one Saturday each month they prepared food and games, and the next day they spent the afternoon entertaining and visiting with the hospital patients.

In May of 1964 the two Goshen youth groups invited the youth groups from several neighboring towns to join them in an evening devoted to a discussion of interfaith marriage, with Father Riley and myself as resource leaders. The fact was stressed that while revolutionary changes are taking place in Catholic-Protestant relations, there remain deep differences between the two in some areas, the most sensitive of which is the area of marriage and family life. Father Riley and I were agreed that young people should consider carefully the problems involved before entering into an interfaith marriage.

During this same period the Ladies Guild of St. Thomas Church and the Women's Fellowship of our church agreed to hold joint meetings from time to time.

The men of the two churches at this time had the opportunity to give an ecumenical twist to the Goshen virtue of neighborly help. The home and business of a young Goshen Protestant couple were completely demolished by a gas explosion. The men of the two churches organized and carried out a public chicken barbeque which netted about one thousand dollars for the couple. In addition a home was provided, readied, and furnished for them by members of both churches.

The following year the laymen of the two churches organized themselves to help a Catholic family in town that had been hit by several serious illnesses and staggering hospital bills. An ecumenical dinner-dance was sponsored by the two churches, and almost $2,500 was turned over to the stricken family.

During this period several members of the two churches suggested that, while it was good to gather together to hear

182

outside experts discuss Catholic-Protestant relations, it would be more helpful if we gathered informally with only Father Riley and myself as resource leaders. They had questions to ask, they said, but they did not want to reveal their ignorance and appear silly before outsiders. Thus, the next step was to initiate what we called the "Open-End Discussion Group." The purpose was to give each person a chance to ask the questions he wanted to ask and to talk about what was on his mind. Also, the group would be open-ended as far as the number of meetings held and the final termination of the group. The group itself would decide when they wanted to meet, what they wanted to talk about, and when they wanted to terminate.

In October of 1964 the Open-End Discussion Group began, and it was at this time that we became aware that all was not roses. There were reservations as well as enthusiasm about ecumenism. There was a longing to be closer to each other, but there was also fear of getting too close. While two or three hundred persons would come out to hear two experts discuss Catholic-Protestant relations, only sixty (thirty Catholic and thirty Protestant) showed up for the intimate face-to-face discussions. Members of both churches suddenly found any number of pressing engagements that prevented them from attending the discussions. Practically no one was so secure in his own faith and in his love for his neighbors that he did not feel threatened by a face-to-face encounter with Christians who had different ideas and viewpoints. Some were afraid of being too stupid and ignorant. Others were afraid of getting angry and being drawn into controversy. A great many just did not want to get that deeply involved in an area that was this sensitive and personal.

At these sessions we would sit around tables—four Protestants and four Catholics per table. The topic for discussion would be decided upon and discussed; then each table would make a report to the rest of the group and quite often ask Father

Riley and me to discuss the topic further. We discussed everything from the authority of the Pope and "saying your beads"
to the place of worship in the life of the church. These meetings
continued every other week from October 1964 until May of
1965.

At the final session of this group each table was requested
to find an answer to the question, "Where do we want to
go next in our Goshen dialogue?" While they were talking
among themselves, Father Riley and I talked, and as we talked,
we decided that we would like to invite the Jewish congregation
in nearby Torrington to join us in a Bible study group. We did
not, however, reveal our wishes to the group. We asked each
table for a report and without any knowledge of what the others
had decided, every one of the groups came up with the same
idea: Let's ask our Jewish brothers to join us in an Old Testament Study Group. Coincidence? Mental telepathy? Or the
work of the Holy Spirit? Whatever the cause, we were delighted
that it was operative, for it led to a very exciting new turn in
the ecumenical movement in the Litchfield Hills of northwestern Connecticut.

In December of 1964 I asked the members of our church
cabinet what they thought about the dialogue. The response
was that we should definitely continue. There were, they
reported, a few persons in town who really were opposed to
the whole thing and quite a few who did not much care one
way or the other. But it was the opinion of these leaders of
our church that the "core" of both churches was solidly behind
the dialogue. Having said this much, however, they went on
with caveats: (1) the dialogue should not be allowed to replace
the group life and activities of our church, and (2) while the
church should be committed to a continuing dialogue, we should
not pressure individuals into being more involved than they
want to be. Each person must be allowed to make his own
response. We agreed that the church must be willing to support

a member when he withdraws in fear and encourage him when he steps forward in response to his yearning.

The Week of Prayer for Christian Unity was again observed in January of 1965. The response was good, but we still had to hold our services of prayer for each other in separate places. It was at this time that Father Riley and I decided to ask Archbishop O'Brien of the Archdiocese of Hartford for permission to hold joint prayer services in 1966.

During the Lenten season of 1965 the two churches sponsored a Lenten seminar series on "The Great Doctrines of the Faith," with William Muehl, professor of practical theology at Yale Divinity School, and Father Frank Dumont, professor of theology at Montfort Seminary, as leaders. The meetings were held on five successive Sunday evenings with an average of 130 to 150 persons in attendance. The five doctrines discussed were the Trinity, the Creation and Fall, the Redemptive Incarnation, the Holy Spirit, and the Fulfillment of Creation. Father Dumont gave the historical development and understanding of each doctrine, and Professor Muehl discussed the meaning of each doctrine for our lives today. The obvious popularity of the series led Father Riley and me to the conclusion that this series would have been an excellent way to have begun the dialogue between the two churches.

In Connecticut there is developing an awareness of the value, even necessity, for regionalism in all areas of community life. Some church leaders, both Catholic and Protestant, are beginning to see that there is a serious hiatus in the church's mission created by the church's organization on a parish level and on a larger jurisdictional level (most often a state-wide organization) with no very effective instrumentalities in between. Thus, in northwestern Connecticut there are Catholic and Protestant churches in each local community, but not one single ecclesiastical body concerned with the needs of persons and communities that could best be met on a regional basis by the cooperative endeavors of several local parishes and communities.

The same is true in the political, economic, and social life of the area. Political leaders are considering very seriously the possibilities of regional planning as are the economic leaders of the area.

We are beginning to see that the Christian church is called to minister to persons, not only in their individual lives and in their lives in groups within the church, but also in their lives in groups outside the church. Thus, we are discovering that the church can have a rewarding and exciting ministry of reconciliation by working with joint labor-management groups and a ministry of healing by working for the establishment of more adequate mental health clinics in the area. The church can give men bread by helping develop the economic resources of our area, and it binds up men's wounds by seeing to it that the area has adequate public health services, that schools have trained personnel to work with the disturbed child (and the disturbed family which produced the child). In such ministries the church can stop being a relief agency and doling out handouts, and start developing the resources of creation, both natural and human, to meet more adequately the needs of persons. In this way the church, as servant of men and the community, can cooperate with the political, economic, and social structures of the region to fulfill its own nature and mission.

Such thinking was the background for the establishment in 1965 of the joint Catholic-Protestant Committee on Regional Planning. The committee is composed of twelve laymen, six from each church, plus Father Riley and myself. The function of the committee is to help prepare the residents of Goshen for participation in a ten-town regional planning body now being formulated. The present purpose is primarily educational. What its function will be if and when the Torrington-Win-chester Planning Region is operative and Goshen is a member remains to be seen. We know only that there is a vast potential ministry in the social structure of the area and that the church needs to be open to the opportunities as they arise. My own hope is that our present, temporary Ecumenical Committee on Regional Planning may eventually be established as a permanent Committee on Social Concern.

In May of 1965 the members of the Open-End Discussion Group had hoped that we could find a way to study the Bible with our Jewish brothers. In October that hope became a reality. Rabbi Abraham Cutler and the members of the Torrington Beth El Synagogue received our invitation with real eagerness. Rabbi Cutler, in addition to his weekend rabbinical duties, is Professor of Talmud Law at the Academy of Higher Jewish Learning, a graduate, rabbinical seminary in New York City. Prior to taking his present position at the institution, Rabbi Cutler had been the leader of several leading synagogues in New York City.

So, at the first session of our joint Torrington Area Jewish-Catholic-Protestant Old Testament Study Group, held in our church and attended by approximately 125 persons from the three congregations, Father Riley and I were somewhat subdued with awe before Rabbi Cutler's erudition. However, this awe soon faded before the excitement generated in our discussion of the first chapters of Genesis. By the time we came to the Adam and Eve stories we were aware of many areas of agreement as well as disagreement. The areas of agreement, we have found, allow us to continue the dialogue while our disagreements add spice and excitement. Most frequently, we have found, the differences between us are apt to be differences born of personal interpretation or of difficulties in finding a common vocabulary. For instance, when we came to the Abrahamic Convenant, we seemed to be poles apart in our understanding of the concept of the covenant God. However, further discussion revealed that we were all trying to say essentially the same thing in different ways. This is not always the case, however. There are genuine and abiding differences between the traditions as we study the same scriptures, and no amount of goodwill will make them go away.

The Old Testament Study Group meets twice monthly on alternate Sunday evenings for two hours. The first hour and a half is devoted to a panel discussion between Rabbi Cutler, Father Riley, and myself, with questions and comments welcomed at any time from the other participants. The last half hour is given over to a coffee break and a time for fellowship. We believe that the coffee and chitchat are as important as the study of scripture. No termination date has been set for the study group. In six months we have covered only the first fifteen chapters of Genesis!

In December of 1965 Archbishop O'Brien gave his approval for joint services of worship during the January, 1966, Week of Prayer for Christian Unity. The services were conducted by Father Riley and myself, assisted by one layman from each of the two churches. Half of the services were conducted in St. Thomas Church and half in ours.

To say that the next event in our continuing dialogue and mutual ministry was a flop would not be exactly fair. It is only honest, however, to report that it failed to reach everyone's expectations. This was our Ecumenical Family Life Workshop held on the four Wednesday evenings of February, 1966. Our resource leaders were Father Randall Blackall, family life director for the Archdiocese of Hartford, and Dr. Russell Becker, associate professor of practical theology at Yale Divinity School. The topics discussed in the four sessions were "Pressures on the Family Today," "The Role of the Church and Family in the Formation of Christian Character," "The Tension Points Within the Family," and "The Christian View of Sex Today."

But the workshop did not quite come off. Almost everyone

said, "Well, it wasn't a complete waste of time, but—!" But
—it could have been a lot better! Perhaps the differences
between the Catholic ethos and the Protestant ethos are too
focused on this extremely sensitive area.

We are now in the midst of a series of studies in sex
education and preparation for courtship and marriage for the
young people of Goshen sponsored by the two churches. The
youth groups themselves suggested the idea and requested
Father Riley and me to set it up for them. The title of the
series, "Fit to Be Tied," comes from the name given by the
Episcopal Church to a program developed for the young people
of that denomination. Local medical doctors, social workers,
psychologists, and Father Riley, and I serve as resource leaders.

Where do we go next in Goshen's continuing ecumenical
dialogue? Father Riley and I agree that the dialogue has not
passed beyond the need for a lot of formal meetings and study
groups, but it seems to be firmly rooted in our community life.
Perhaps the watering and tending of the new plant is no
longer necessary. It is no longer something that needs to be
cultivated but, rather, is a form of the church's ministry that
needs to be used. It is being used now to express the concern
of all Goshen Christians for those who experience a time of
trouble, and it is being used to carry out the church's ministry
to persons through the structures of society in the work of the
Joint Committee on Regional Planning. It will be used when
we begin a series of studies for parents on the sex education
of children. We hope to use it also in the "Living Room
Dialogues" which we intend to set up, and on those occasions
when we will get together for worship and fellowship and
together rediscover the deeply satisfying and heartening fact
that while there is yet much that separates us, there is also
much that unites us. Perhaps most of all we pray that each one
of us will see even more clearly that the "much that unites
us" is really "he who unites us."

18

Senior Citizens' Fellowship

Oliver deW. Cummings

It was evident that something imaginative needed to be done at First Baptist. The "battle of Los Angeles," as some of the church leaders were facetiously calling it, was becoming each day more difficult—and challenging.

Already, through its long history from the early beginnings of the little pueblo of "the Angeles," the church had faced many changes and, by 1956, had established itself as one of the strong, metropolitan churches of the country. A magnificent building with some 120 rooms, located in the heart of the Wilshire area, was serving as the spiritual home base for a widely diversified ministry in this sprawled out megopolis. The program included many elements of strength, designed to serve the real needs of real persons—an outstanding pulpit ministry, a strong emphasis upon music and worship, an excellent, thoroughly graded and well-staffed church school, a Saturday club program for children, including skating units in the gym and choir units in the music center, a well-rounded youth program. Also, the church enjoyed a reputation for friendliness and concern for persons.

Many pilot projects had been attempted with varying success, but the members and leaders were not satisfied. A plateau had been reached statistically—a leveling off and then a decline. The staff and the members were concerned. Was there to be for the church a beautiful sunset or a bright sunrise full of hope? What should be done to serve the needs of people in the inner city when more and more of the active members were moving to remote suburbs?

Already the national Home Mission Society had, upon the church's invitation, sent its task force to survey and appraise the needs, trends, and potentialities of the situation in the changing city and had helped the church to evaluate the strengths and weaknesses of its current program and to consider recommendations concerning the future. "These studies," said one church leader, "confirm judgments which we have already made at many points. They give us a solid factual base for many of our opinions. And they represent a few surprises."

A strongly confirmed judgment was the belief that there were large numbers of senior adults in the Wilshire area and that the church should undertake a special senior citizen ministry. The church's minister of education was asked to add this to his other duties. He was given an undefined assignment, no budget or ready-made staff of helpers, and encouraged to experiment. This is exactly what he did.

Steps were taken to get started—appointment by the Church Council of a joint committee of the Board of Deacons and the Board of Education, interviews with leaders already involved in clubs and activities for seniors in Los Angeles city, county, and elsewhere, assignments to several persons to gather data about needs, potentialities, and guidance principles. Hopeful approaches to potential leaders of committees were greeted with typical reactions—"I'm glad something is being attempted, but don't count on me to help"; "I don't have that kind of ability"; "I don't have time"; "I'll do what I can"; and a few yeses. Leaders were named, a date was set, and a pilot project announced—once a week on Wednesday afternoons between Easter and summer. The Senior Citizens' Fellowship, as it was called, was on its way.

A few basic assumptions and guiding principles were established, some "hunches" were followed, and a period of experimentation—trial and error, failure and success—was begun. The road to be traveled was toward a vibrant, person-centered ministry in which adults of all faiths, races, and stations in life might find impetus to creative living. The going was slow at first, and results not easy.

One naïve assumption—that adults outside the church were eagerly waiting for an opportunity to flood into the church building and would come without much personal contact—soon proved to be fallacious. Another assumption, that senior church members had time on their hands, was found to be equally fallacious. Most church members, it was found, were already in their own minds "too busy," and many nonchurch members interpreted the activities as merely another clever way of getting new "joiners" for the church, not an evidence of genuine interest. Typical reactions were, "Oh, I'm not ready for that, yet," or "I'm a Lutheran . . . Methodist . . Catholic . . of the Jewish faith."

In spite of disappointments and some early mistakes the initial experiment was a success. Later developments have made this one of the most exciting missionary outreach and service ministries in the church's history. Beginning with twenty-five to fifty persons, most of them already related to the church, the number grew to "several hundred," "over a thousand," and then climbed to approximately three thousand—the great majority of these, possibly ninety percent, not otherwise related to the church. Beginning with one activity weekly, the program grew to include an extensive schedule of classes, forums, luncheons, musical entertainments, fun programs, and lectures and movies on health, travel, Bible study, and many other themes.

A first trip—to the county fair—timidly undertaken with one busload expanded to as many as ten busloads (four hundred people) and a regular tour schedule: *Trip of the Month* (to nearby places), *Overnighters* (to such places as Death Valley, Monterey, Yosemite, San Francisco, Grand Canyon, Carlsbad, Lake Tahoe, New England, the Seattle and New York World's Fairs), and *International Good Neighbor Tours* (to the Caribbean, Mexico, Canada, the Orient, Europe, and the Holy Land).

An "orbit of living" has been presented to adults in retiremnet and preretirement years which includes mental and spiritual enrichment, study and education, housing, health, travel, recreation, and meaningful service. Adults in considerable numbers are responding. The church's ministry is greatly expanding, its building and facilities finding many constructive uses, its good name and influence spreading, and new senior adults are joining the church.

The spoken and written comments of appreciation have been gratifying. For instance, "I come in tired and discouraged; I go out walking on air." "I feel like a schoolgirl again" [ninety-year-old on trip]. "From week to week I live for these meetings." "I come here because I feel so safe." "An apartment in a big city can be a very lonely place, but here loneliness vanishes into thin air." "When my husband died, I don't know how I could have made it without this activity [Learn-to-Paint class] and these friends." "I've had a new lease on life." "Because of the fellowship—what we have done and seen—the two years since we retired have been the happiest years of our lives" [a married couple]. "I have met here the dearest friends of my life, and I am grateful to you." Such personal testimonials make the effort expended in planning programs, trips, and projects seem well worthwhile.

It is the human element which has made the difference— the person-to-person, word-of-mouth sharing of delight in the discovery that many of the problems of city living, scatteration, depersonalization, anonymity, loneliness, can be overcome when people care enough to share. The result is a full-orbited program touching in meaningful ways some three thousand people in varied activities and services. Much more—here is a living demonstration that city living in our modern day can provide many comforts, conveniences, and advantages when the spirit of him who looked upon the multitudes with compassion is applied to an all-out effort to assure abundant living in mature years and as long as God gives breath.

The senior citizen friends of First Baptist, outside and inside the membership of the church, have become an active missionary force to sing the praises of the church wherever they go throughout Los Angeles and to invite friends and neighbors to participate in its activities. It is doubtless true that more persons are being reached in more different ways in this department of the church than in any other. An encouraging development has likewise been an increasing number attending the Sunday services and joining the church, though at the outset it was determined that results would be measured by service to people in the spirit of Christ, rather than by the number joining the church. As one enthusiastic booster said, "I made up my mind after finding so many nice people from this church on the bus trips, that there must be something very special about the church itself. So I started attending on Sundays and found this to be true. Now I am very happy that I can call this 'my church.'"

One evidence that the program is rendering service is the schedule of diverse activities, added one by one, to meet consciously expressed needs. For example, one monthly mailing announced the following:

MONDAYS

    10:00—Service sewing groups: Red Cross, Dorcas, White Cross

Senior Citizens' Fellowship

WEDNESDAYS

10:00—Learn to Paint, Wood Carving classes
6:00—Church dinner

THURSDAYS

10:00—Class on "Creative Living—the Art of Keeping Alive and Alert"

FRIDAYS

9:00—Speech reading (Classes for those with hearing loss)
Music appreciation class

10:00—"American Problems and World Affairs" (Discussion Class)
Chorus singing—class

SPECIAL EVENTS—JUNE

3rd—1:00 P.M. Forum #1: "The Communist Bloc— Czechoslovakia and Hungary."

10th—1:00 P.M. Forum #2: "The Communist Block— Rumania and Bulgaria."

17th—12:00 NOON. Commencement Luncheon: Mexican Fiesta—songs, entertainment, travelogue.

19th—11:00 A.M. Commissioning of "World Neighbor Ambassadors" (those participating in three international "Good Neighbor Tours" to Mexico, Canadian Rockies, and Alaska, via Canada) at the Sunday morning worship service.

24th—11:00 A.M. "Good Old Summer Time." Programs: Songs of Merry England, Bonnie Scotland, Dear Old Ireland.
1:00 P.M. Armchair Trip: England, Scotland, and Ireland.

28th—"Ports of Call" trip—San Pedro.

Organizationally, the Senior Citizens' Fellowship, a recognized department of the church's activity, is guided by a council of some twenty-five members made up about evenly of representatives of church boards, adult classes and organizations, and "coordinators" selected from the participating units and activities. It functions through three units which work together to produce a well-rounded, integrated program.

The units are (1) the Go Club, concerned primarily with trips; (2) the Wayfinders' Club, concerned with hearing and health; (3) the XYZ (Zest) Club (Extra Years of Zest), providing luncheons, meetings, classes, forums, interest groups, and service projects.

Financially, the Senior Citizens had been a distinct asset, being entirely on a self-support basis, including the full salary of the full-time minister of senior citizens, the part-time hostess-registrar, and two part-time office secretaries, besides contributing to many church improvements and directly to the church expenses and to missions. Funds are raised from membership fees, voluntary donations, and service charges on trips.

THE UNDERLYING PHILOSOPHY OF NEIGHBORLINESS

Very early in the planning, the concept of "neighborliness" emerged as the unifying philosophy and the central objective. Later the spectacular growth had been accompanied by a broadening of scope and deepening of aims. These aims were eventually formulated into a series of recommendations, labeled "Brief #1," presented to the Church Council for study and action, and have served since as a blueprint for program building. They are as follows:

Brief #1—*Recommendations for Study and Action*

I. That a GOOD NEIGHBOR CENTER be established at the First Baptist Church for the purpose of rendering neighborly services to senior citizens and others and of enlisting the financial and human resources of time, money, and skill of senior citizens and others in constructive projects of neighborliness—local, national, and worldwide.

II. That this GOOD NEIGHBOR CENTER include the following:

1. *The Adult Community Center* of the First Baptist Church, with its senior citizens' office, dining room, kitchens, class and assembly halls, social hall and gym, adult activity center, "World Neighbor Lounge," and other facilities.

2. *A Retirement Home* or apartment building, built over the present parking lot, continuing to make available the present parking facilities for use by the church and the Adult Community Center.

3. *A Health Center or Infirmary* (or both of these) to provide limited care and assistance to residents of the Retirement Home not needing hospitalization, and to senior citizens and others needing limited help. For example: hearing tests (such as those already conducted for senior citizens and preschool-age children), mental health and counseling (such as already being provided through the Guidance Center of the First Baptist Church), lectures and movies on diet and health, and many others. Likewise available might be a resident physician or a referral office for arranging house calls for persons needing a visiting nurse or doctor.

4. Such other building or facilities for health, housing or recreation as may be required by an expanding program.

III. That a GOOD NEIGHBOR PROGRAM be established, including the following:

1. *Educational*—classes, lectures, forums (including adult education classes of city schools); *Good Neighbor Center Publications*—leaflets, manuals, and books for distribution locally and nationally, and through the *Good Neighbor Circulating Library and Reading Room.*

2. *Health and Medicare*—as outlined above.

3. *Housing*—as outlined above.

4. *Recreation*—luncheons, picnics, parties, game room, movies, music, entertainments.

5. *Trips and Travel*—Go-Club "Day Trips," "Overnighters," and "Internationals."

6. *World Peace Projects* of many types, enlisting the creative abilities, skills, and financial support of retired persons.

7. *Person-to-Person Ministries*—"Lend-a-Hand" Plan, "Phone Pals," "Bridges of Friendship" emphases.

IV. That a GOOD NEIGHBOR FOUNDATION be established to publicize projects, receive gifts and bequests, establish relationships with other foundations or trusts and supervise the expenditure of allocations in compliance with the wishes of donors.

THE GOOD NEIGHBOR CENTER

Most of the items in "Brief #1" have now gone far beyond the drawing board stage and are actually in partial or full operation. The conversion of the Adult Community Center to the Good Neighbor Center, as a congenial activity area for senior citizens, required few structural changes but many improvements in decorations and equipment. In these changes the seniors themselves contributed hundreds of man-hours of labor with paint brushes, scaffolding, carpenter's tools, and several thousands of dollars for basic improvements and items of equipment. When an adult classroom needed to be converted into a Senior citizens' office and the former Youth Center to the Adult Activity Center, the wide, lower hallway into the World Neighbor Lounge, and a large storage room into a workroom and stack room for the Good Neighbor Library, the seniors were ready. Walls and ceilings were painted, display panels mounted, cabinets and counters built, a new doorway cut through, asphalt tile installed—all by volunteer senior citizens' labor with cash donations covering much of the cost for paint, lumber, and tile. A retired telephone repairman made electrical repairs and improvements. The church provided modern lighting and an elevator. The seniors raised money for coffee makers and thermos pitchers, portable amplifiers and loudspeakers for a donated record player for music programs in the World Neighbor Lounge, and an overhead projector for the speech-reading class.

In the firm conviction that almost any church or club house has some room which may serve as an attractive and friendly place for seniors to meet and that every meeting place of senior adults throughout America should become a Good Neighbor Center, the Senior Citizens' Fellowship is launching a movement to enlist charter members in a chain of Good Neighbor Centers committed to a few common approaches to interfaith, inter-racial, and international understanding and neighborly self-help projects for community betterment and world peace.

A two-year preliminary feasibility study of a proposed high-rise retirement home has resulted in church action to create a nonprofit corporation to proceed further with the review of this project. It is apparent that there are many older people who wish to enjoy the comforts, conveniences, and opportunities for enjoyment and enrichment in the heart of a great city, "close to everything." Such a housing project as part of a Good Neighbor Center, with other housing developments for young adults, international students, and newcomers from other countries might well provide a major answer to the problem of creating a dynamic, living community in the very midst of the city.

The Good Neighbor Center has continued to provide weekly classes in speech reading for adults with hearing loss and is lending its support, as a pilot project, to the development of teaching films. It is also investigating proposals looking toward establishing a five-day-a-week school for practice in speech-reading, associated with opportunities to mingle with others in classes and activities and to stimulate improvement. Free hearing tests for preliminary screening have been furnished to several hundred adults with trained audiometrists and professionally qualified counselors. Lectures on medicare, health, and diet have been offered at regular intervals.

THE GOOD NEIGHBOR PROGRAM

A program of variety and appeal has been offered based upon returns from questionnaires, brainstorming sessions, and straw votes. One of the strongest parts of the program is educational —classes, lectures, and forums. And here the Los Angeles city school system has proved to be a strong ally through its adult education program, pioneered by Dr. Ann Morgan Barron. Dr. Barron developed courses of particular interest to older people and promoted the idea that adult education classes should find their way into churches, hotels, retirement homes, or other places where older people gather. The church or other facility provides rent-free space greatly needed by the public schools. The sponsoring agent provides the people, the spirit, and the enthusiasm that make for enjoyable and effective learning.

The church has helped the city schools to keep the classes and forums strongly related to the real needs and interest of older people as well as academically sound. For example, the discussion class on "American Problems and World Affairs" deals from week to week with headline news from all parts of the world as well as local problems of citizenship and of senior adults.

The profile of the course on gerontology, announced as "Creative Living—the Art of Keeping Alive and Alert," reads like a summary of objectives of the senior citizens' movement itself. It is no wonder that the reactions are so enthusiastic. Here is a description of the course:

A self-improvement workshop dealing with physical and mental health and personal appearance, personality development and enrichment, poise, posture and charm, maintaining vitality and radiance, keeping fit and attractive, calisthenics, good grooming and neatness, fads and fashions, diet and nutrition, budgeting and meal planning, acquiring skills and interests, finding new areas of enjoyment, cultivating your sense of humor, getting along with yourself and with others, making the most of your potentialities.

Best attended of the programs have been the monthly luncheons and the Adult Community Center Forums, with motion pictures, lectures, and discussion covering such topics as the Caribbean, the Mediterranean, Africa, Asia, Western Europe, the Island World of the Pacific, Long Red Shadows of the Bamboo Curtain, and Countries Inside the Iron Curtain.

Good Neighbor Publications have appeared on such topics as Spiritual Exercises, Pointers on Neighborliness, Thanksgiving, Peace on Earth, Contented Living Quotations, God Speaks, a Peace Charter, a Senior Citizen, and a series of Good Neighbor Song Sheets—Songs of Bonnie Scotland, Patriotic Songs of America, Songs of Dear Old Ireland, Canadian and U.S.A. Songs.

The Good Neighbor Library and the World Neighbor Lounge, adjoining each other, have become centers for emphasis upon the heritage of music, art and craftsmanship, literature, history, and the creative achievement of many lands and peoples. Here flags have been dedicated to countries visited in Good Neighbor Tours, posters and paintings are displayed, recordings are played, art objects and missionary curios from different lands are displayed. Also the world mission of the church is dramatized here and a meeting point furnished for missionary-minded church members and world-minded citizens. Financial projects arising out of Good Neighbor Tours have included such missionary work as Haiti, Mexico, and the Church World Service in Hong Kong.

The Person-to-Person Good Neighbor Ministries have stressed many personal contacts with the sick, the shut-ins, and the lonely. Each week a stream of individuals—some very much in need of friendship and inspiration—flow into and out of the building. Most find help, strength, and joy in living; many find real spiritual uplift. There are many pastoral and counseling opportunities. After all, the great needs are psychological and spiritual—the need to be needed and cherished, the need for freedom from fear, for faith in time of suffering and loss, the assurance that "the best is yet to be" because "our times are in the hands of one" who has planned for the rhythm of life, childhood, youth, adulthood, and maturity, and also for life beyond death.

A Good Neighbor Corps has been initiated, providing opportunity for enlistment for volunteer services as Willing Workers (the mailing crew), Fix-Things-Uppers (painting, repair work, and odd jobs), Doorbell Ringers (distributing literature, calling on shut-ins, etc.) and Phone Pals. Ultimately there is envisioned, if incoming funds permit, the commissioning of corps members with specialized skills as consultants for short-term assignments.

A good start toward the Good Neighbor Fund has been made through gifts from the contributing, supporting, sponsoring, and patron members. In addition legacies and capital gifts are encouraged, and some of these have been received. The fulfillment of the ultimate dream of a substantial endowment to underwrite constructive projects of neighborliness—local, national, and worldwide—still lies ahead.

As cherished dreams are being fulfilled and new plans being shaped, the future is bright with promise. It is evident that a spiritually oriented, rather than a secularly based, program is more in step with the ultimate needs of maturing adults and can enlist their active participation and tangible support. There is great hope that the senior citizens' movement may achieve stature by accepting a cause—the simple but profound objective of neighborliness—as its central purpose and that hands may be linked together across America and around the globe for world peace and cooperation. Wherever there are senior adults, few or many, the church has a mission to perform, a force to be enlisted for peace on earth and goodwill among men. This is the vision and the faith of the Good Neighbor Center at First Baptist, Los Angeles.

EDITORS and CONTRIBUTORS

WILLIAM N. ASWAD was born in Binghamton, New York. He is a graduate of Clarkson College of Technology, with a B.A. degree in chemical engineering. He is employed by the General Electric Company in the field of manufacturing engineering. His home is in Burlington, Vermont.

PAUL C. CARTER, JR., is a native of Rochester, New York. He has earned degrees from Bucknell University (A.B.), Colgate Rochester Divinity School (B.D.), and Union Theological Seminary (S.T.M.). He was the pastor of the Church of St. John the Baptist, Bronx, New York, and is currently resource minister for the New York City Neighborhood Ministries Project. Mr. Carter's home is in the Bronx.

M. EDWARD CLARK was born in Kenton, Ohio. He has his B.A. from the College of Wooster, his B.D. from Colgate Rochester Divinity School, his M.A. from Hartford School of Religious Education, Hartford Seminary Foundation, and his Ed.R.D. from the Hartford Seminary Foundation. He has published a number of articles in religious periodicals. Mr. Clark was formerly the consultant in Christian education for the Connecticut Council of Churches. He is presently professor of religious education at the Central Baptist Theological Seminary, Kansas City, Kansas.

KENNETH W. CONNERS was born in Minotola, New Jersey. He has degrees from Wharton School, the University of Pennsylvania (B.S. in economics), the University of Pennsylvania (A.M.), and has done additional study at the Psychological Clinic of the University of Pennsylvania, at Temple University, and at Mansfield College, Oxford. Mr. Conners has published articles in publications such as *American Mercury, American Photography, Christian Advocate,* and *The London Studio.* He is the author of the book *Pro, Con, and Coffee.* Mr. Conners is vice-president of the Philadelphia Science Council, director and member of the executive committee of the Greater Philadelphia Council of Churches, and a leader in his home church—First Methodist Church of Germantown, Pennsylvania. He is manager of the advertising division, Leeds & Northrup Company, Philadelphia.

MARY F. CRAWFORD was born in Nevada, Missouri. She has a B.S. in education from the State College of Springfield, Missouri, an M.A. in education from the University of Missouri, and she has done graduate work at Drake University. She has been a kindergarten teacher in the public schools of Des Moines, Iowa, and is at the present time a teacher of the trainable mentally retarded in the Des Moines school system. Miss Crawford has published articles in the *International Journal of Religious Education* and in the *Baptist Leader*.

OLIVER deW. CUMMINGS is a native of Chester, Pennsylvania. He has a B.A. from University of Redlands, a B.D. and M.R.E. from Andover Newton Theological School. He has received an honorary D.D. from the University of Redlands. He has written a number of books among which are: *Administering Christian Education in the Local Church* and *Guiding Youth in Christian Growth*. He has been the national director of youth work for the American Baptist Convention and the director of Christian education and youth work for the Southern California Baptist Convention. At the present time he is the minister of senior citizens, First Baptist Church, Los Angeles, California.

R. EDWARD DOWDY was born in Rocky Mount, Virginia. He is a graduate of Roanoke College in Salem, Virginia, and of the Colgate Rochester Divinity School (B.D.) He is a frequent contributor to the *Baptist Leader* and is the author of *The Church Is Families*. He has been vice-president of the American Baptist board of education and publication. Mr. Dowdy was the pastor of the Woodruff Place Baptist Church in Indianapolis, Indiana, and is presently the pastor of the Emmanuel Baptist Church in Brooklyn, New York.

JOHN C. GARVIN is a native of Finleyville, Pennsylvania. He received his A.B. from the University of Pittsburgh and his B.D. from Pittsburgh Theological Seminary. He has been a Presbyterian pastor and is now an elder in The Methodist Church. He is director of the Bethany Ministry, Northview Heights, Pittsburgh, Pennsylvania.

CHARLES W. GELBACH was born in Duncannon, Pennsylvania. He earned his B.A. at Ursinus College and his B.D. at Lancaster Theological Seminary. He is the associate minister and minister of Christian education of the First Congregational Church, Madison, Connecticut.

WILLIAM R. GRACE is a native of Philadelphia, Pennsylvania. He graduated with an A.B. from Catawba College, Salisbury, North Carolina, a B.D. from Princeton Theological Seminary, and an M.A. from the University of Delaware. He has published articles in *Crossroads, McCormick Quarterly,* and in the book *The Church and the Exploding Metropolis.* Mr. Grace was formerly the pastor of the First and Olivet United Presbyterian Church, Wilmington, Delaware, and is at the present time the director of the department of urban church, North Coastal Area, Synod of California, United Presbyterian Church in the U.S.A. (offices in San Francisco, California).

C. LOREN GRAHAM was born in Crete, Nebraska. He has an A.B. from Doane College, a M.Sc. and Ph.D. from the University of Nebraska. He has published a number of scientific and technical articles. Mr. Graham is supervisor, motion picture section, photographic technology division of Eastman Kodak Company, Rochester, New York. He is a fellow in the Society of Motion Picture and Television Engineers.

JANETTE T. HARRINGTON was born in Logan, Ohio. She has a B.S. in journalism from Ohio State University School of Journalism and an M.A. from Teachers College, Columbia University. She has published a number of articles in *Presbyterian Life* and is the author of *The Shadows They Cast, Look at the City,* and *Who Cares?* (coauthored with Muriel Webb). Miss Harrington was formerly employed by the United Presbyterian Board of National Missions and is presently with the Counseling Center of Lewis and Clark College in Portland, Oregon.

REUEL L. HOWE is a native of the state of Washington. He has earned degrees from Whitman College (B.A.), the Divinity School of the Protestant Episcopal Church, Philadelphia (S.T.B., S.T.M., S.T.D.), and an honorary D.D. from Whitman College and from the Chicago Theological Seminary. He has written a number of books including *Herein Is Love, The Creative Years,* and *The Miracle of*

Dialogue. He was formerly on the faculty of the Protestant Episcopal Theological Seminary in Virginia and is presently the director of the Institute for Advanced Pastoral Studies, Bloomfield Hills, Michigan.

J. THOMAS LEAMON is a native of Salem, Massachusetts. He earned his B.F.A. from Rhode Island School of Design, his B.D. from Hartford Seminary Foundation, and he has done additional study at Chicago Theological Seminary and Mansfield College, Oxford. He has contributed articles to the *International Journal of Religious Education* and the *United Church Herald.* He is the author, narrator, and photographer of the color and sound filmstrip *Modern Art and the Gospel.* Mr. Leamon was formerly the pastor of the Westfield Congregational Church in Danielson, Connecticut. He is at the present time the pastor of the First Congregational Church in Williamstown, Massachusetts.

PAUL R. LONG, JR., was born in Wilkes-Barre, Pennsylvania. He has his A.B. from Union College and his B.D. from Yale University Divinity School. He was the pastor of the Lakeside Presbyterian Church in Rochester, New York. He is now the assistant minister of the Third Presbyterian Church, Rochester, New York.

WILLIAM L. MALCOMSON is a native of Cuba, New York. He earned his B.A. from Denison University, his B.D. from Colgate Rochester Divinity School, and his M.A. and Ph.D. from Princeton University. He has published articles in the *Central Baptist Seminary Journal.* He was formerly the pastor of the First Baptist Church of Mansfield, Storrs, Connecticut, and minister to Baptist students at the University of Connecticut. He is presently associate professor of pulpit ministry at the Central Baptist Theological Seminary, Kansas City, Kansas.

WARREN LANE MOLTON was born in Floral City, Florida. He has a B.S. from Wofford College, a B.D. from Southern Baptist Theological Seminary, and an S.T.M. from Yale Divinity School. He has published articles and poems in *The Christian Century* and in denominational periodicals. He was formerly the director of the University Christian Fellowship at the University of Connecticut, Storrs, Connecticut. He is now the associate professor of parish ministry and field education at the Central Baptist Theological Seminary, Kansas City, Kansas.

RAYMOND C. PHIBBS is a native of Pulaski, Virginia. He is a graduate of Bridgewater College, and he earned his B.D. from Yale University Divinity School. He has published a number of articles in denominational periodicals. Mr. Phibbs is pastor of the Church of Christ, Congregational, Goshen, Connecticut.

ARTHUR L. REED was born in Bluffton, Indiana. He earned his B.M. and B.M.Ed. from the Indiana University School of Music, his B.D. from the Hartford Seminary Foundation, and he has done graduate study at the Yale Graduate School of Music. Mr. Reed has been the pastor of the New Castle Congregational Church, New Castle, New Hampshire, and is presently the minister of Christian education, Newtown Congregational Church, Newtown, Connecticut.

DAVID C. RICH is a native of Syracuse, New York. He has a B.A. from Denison University and a B.D. from Andover Newton Theological School. He has been the minister of community service of the Madison Avenue Baptist Church in New York City and is now the eastern director of the Department of Campus Christian Life of the American Baptist Convention.

ROBERT W. SHAFFER was born in Altoona, Pennsylvania. He has a B.A. from Wheaton College and a B.D. from Princeton Theological Seminary. He is the minister of Word and Sacraments of the First Presbyterian Church, Glassboro, New Jersey.